Home-Based Jobs & Sustainable Crafts

*Key Knowledge You Need to Acquire
Now to Understand Basic Economics,
Make Organic Money, and Profit in
Today's Hotter World*

Clement Harrison

Do **NOT** continue reading before you watch <u>this 7-minute video</u>... or you will regret it!

Discover the <u>ESSENTIAL CONCEPTS OF ECONOMICS</u> that everyone needs to know within 7-minutes

<u>This 7-minute video</u> will give you a powerful edge over everyone else by:

- Discovering how to <u>leverage economic tools</u>

- Making you <u>understand our spending habits</u>

- <u>Predicting</u> economic <u>human behavior</u>

- <u>Understanding the markets</u> and the macro economy

professional before attempting any techniques outlined in this book.

By reading this document, the reader agrees that under no circumstances is the author responsible for any losses, direct or indirect, that are incurred as a result of the use of the information contained within this document, including, but not limited to, errors, omissions, or inaccuracies.

Table of Contents

Introduction

Entrepreneurship is the word of the month these days and everyone is looking for the pot of gold at the end of the proverbial rainbow. You only need to scroll through the internet to see just how many get-rich-quick schemes and work from home offers there are out there. Ideas and guidelines on how to start a home-based business are peppered throughout social media so often that it is not only becoming hard to miss, but everyone wants a piece of the entrepreneurial pie. While almost all seem legitimate, some just seem too hard to believe, and not all of the information offered can be useful in the long term.

Now, who wouldn't want to make a little money on the side with a small business? It can give you that little bit of extra cash you need to ease your financial burdens. There are several reasons why people consider starting their businesses: freedom, tax breaks, and having a meaningful life being some of them. Businesses are started for very different reasons by very different people. Entrepreneurship is known to be so successful that there is no reason not to start one. If you're thinking about taking that leap into the business world, then do it, it could be life-changing.

How about thinking a little bigger than just some extra cash, how about turning this into a fully-fledged and lucrative business? It all starts with you, your talents and abilities, your time and effort, as well as what your dreams are for your future. The problem that most people have when trying to start a business is that they don't have a clear, well-thought-out plan to sustain it. Financing is not always readily available, and financial jargon can seem impossible to parse, so they give up. You cannot make money without understanding money. This is the key to starting and sustaining a home-based business.

Business-minded people and small business owners are becoming more environmentally conscious, and many of them have started working to ensure that their products are eco-friendly as well. Starting a home-based, environmentally friendly business is the way to go. Eco-friendly start-up businesses can include anything from supplying products to offering services. People are becoming more aware of the negative effects most large companies have on our environment, so you can use this to your advantage by positioning your business as a friend of the earth and thus attracting customers. Your passion and enthusiasm for the environment will be a calling card to like-minded people, so not only will you be taking care of the earth, but you will also be building a strong business from it.

In this book, we will combine your dream of starting a small, environmentally friendly home-based business, with basic economic principles that can be applied to your business. You will discover how to use the economy to your advantage, thereby putting you miles ahead of others. Understanding the economy and how it works will add considerable value to your business, and you will learn how to reap the benefits of financial success. You have to get the foundation of your business right before you can build on it. Your time is your greatest resource, and investing your time into building a strong foundation by understanding the fundamental principles that drive the market will be the key to your success.

My name is Clement Harrison. I am a professor of Neuroeconomics and a personal development coach. Numerous people from all walks of life read my material to discover how to use psychology and systematic methods to unlock the door to business and personal success. That could mean finding a job you love, earning more money, starting your business or mastering the intricacies of your mind. Even though teaching brings me great joy and students have appreciated the way I have taught them, my greatest passion in life is to see them use what they've learned to become successful in their own lives. This has inspired me to start my very own management consulting firm. My passion has always been to help people become successful by teaching them how to use psychology and systematic methods to their benefit. Anyone can improve their life by becoming someone who can make a difference in today's world.

By the time you come to the end of this book, you will have a greater understanding of how the world works and how the economy functions within it. This knowledge will give you a head start in starting your own business and creating your own wealth. Apply the principles found in this book to your business to make it sustainable and profitable. Help heal the planet and generate a steady stream of income for yourself.

I have received testimonies and words of gratitude from many people saying that these economic principles have helped them not only to look at money differently but to use what they've learned to give them an edge in the business world. They've made subtle changes that have had a great impact on the sustainability of their businesses and in their private lives. I will unveil these same principles to you in this book, principles that are easy to implement and to follow through on.

With my help and knowledge, you will be fully equipped with the skills needed to create or sustain a thriving business. This book will provide support to maintain your time and money while increasing productivity and profits as you build a stable and relevant business. Being able to sustain a business in today's world while ensuring you have a lifetime of wealth is all about discipline and hard work.

Wealth is unlimited and is waiting for someone to reach out and grab it. Time, however, is not. We all have a small window of time given to us, how we use this will determine how successful we become. Sustainable businesses have untapped potential for profit and could result in reversing global warming. Being a responsible business owner in today's world will help you build a strong customer base with those who share the same principles as yourself. There is a huge market for eco-friendly businesses, where you can do your part for the environment without affecting your bottom line.

There is no better time than now to get started. Fulfill your dreams of building a sustainable business and having a lifetime of wealth. You can do all this without leaving a carbon footprint. The economic principles you are about to read are proven facts. The actionable steps identified in this book will yield incredible results for anyone choosing to apply them. Every chapter is packed with knowledge and guidelines that will enhance your business, taking it to the next level. Your perspective on life and the world around you will be changed, allowing you to be more receptive to making sustainability a reality.

Work from home. Make money fast. Save the planet.

Chapter 1:
The Secret to
Understanding How the
Pricing System Works

Supply and Demand

Supply and demand is a theory used in economics that explains how the supply of and demand for goods and services affects the pricing. When the demand for goods is higher than the supply, the price of said goods goes up, however, when the supply of goods is higher than the demand, the price of the goods goes down. In most cases, if an item's price is far too high, even if there is a demand for it, most consumers will not pay for it. The company then has to lower the price to sell the product. The price of goods also has a significant effect on demand. The higher the price of something, the less demand there is for it. On the other hand, when the product is priced cheaper, the product demand for it will increase.

While this is the general rule of supply and demand, there may be other factors that can influence the cost of products and services.

Sometimes cost can be affected by the public's perception of what could happen in the future. For instance, if they think that there will be a shortage of something, this will increase the demand and lead companies to increase their prices. These prices could be inflated by more than 100%.

There are also cases where the supply and demand of certain products do not have an effect on their price or sales in the market. A notable example occurs when companies do not allow you to bring your own food, snacks, or beverages onto their premises, leaving you with no option but to purchase them. This allows the companies to inflate their food and drink prices so much that they are far more expensive than they would be if you bought them elsewhere. These companies can do this because they've created an environment in which there is no competition. Competitive business practices typically serve to correct irregularities in the supply and demand theory. However, there are times when the government may intervene and set a fixed price on goods. Price control can work against the supplier, especially if the price is so low that the demand becomes too high for the supplier to meet, leaving consumers waiting for far too long before the demand is met.

The law of supply and demand affects not only tangible products but also other areas of the economy. Banks are continually adjusting interest rates to increase or decrease the demand for the supply of money. When the interest rates are low, lots more people borrow money, this increases spending and productivity, which lifts the economy. When interest rates are higher, people are dissuaded from spending their money. They tend to save it instead. The Federal Reserve bank has the power to influence the economy by decreasing the interest rates, thus allowing the price of assets to increase and creating employment opportunities. Although the number of assets remains the same during inflation and deflation, the lower rates foster demand for these assets, which increases the cost of the assets. In the same way, high rates decrease the demand for these assets, pushing the price down. Consumers continuously have to adjust the way they spend their money based solely on the decisions of others.

Market Forces

There is a considerable demand for goods or services. The population's demand for things and their availability is not equal. You don't even need to look further than your very own town to see that not everyone's needs are being met. There is only a limited amount of resources available to meet the needs of everyone. The reason that resources are limited is not because there isn't enough to go around. The reason is that we consume far more than we need. This, in turn, leaves those who are not quick or can't afford something with empty hands.

Our society is made up of individuals who are eager to better themselves and individuals who are willing to use someone else's talents to their advantage. This creates a market for one's talents and a willingness to pay for it. For example, if you need a bookcase, but you don't have the skill to make one, you will pay someone who has the ability to build one. This exchange is mutually advantageous and both of you will benefit from this arrangement.

A market is created between individuals who can benefit from each other. Each person is free to choose who he wants to transact with over numerous commodities. He can even choose not to transact at all. It must be understood that economic principles and laws have a significant influence on the market.

Economic theory depends mainly on the feelings and needs of humans. Hunger increases the demand for food; learning increases the demand for books. Human beings are free to choose based on how attractive something appears to them. We tend to choose things that will add value to our lives. Economic theorists study this behavior and then try and predict what will happen in the real world. They try to explain the ripple effect that the change in prices in one market may have on other areas in the market. If a product is in short supply, similar and cheaper versions of this product could be sold at a higher than standard cost.

Elasticity and Government Policy

Price elasticity is a phenomenon that can impact the shifts in a product's supply and demand. Understanding price elasticity will show you how the price of some goods is affected. Certain necessities have a steady price like housing and cars, etc., then there are non-essentials such as eating out that can fluctuate in price. The government uses price elasticity to determine the tax placed on some goods.

Let's take coffee beans as an example. This is the main product of coffee shops. If the government lowers taxes on coffee beans, The coffee shop can choose to decrease the customer's price for coffee depending on the elasticity of demand. A high demand elasticity means that a decrease in the price of coffee causes the demand for coffee to increase at such a high rate that the coffee shop owner can earn more profit at a lower price than the higher price. Benefitting both the coffeeshop owner and the customers

Efficiency of Markets

When money is invested in the stock market, the goal is not only to make more money but also to outperform and beat the market. The amounts reflected in the market are based on all the available information at any given time. Because no one has information that is not yet available, it is unlikely that an investor can predict a return on the stock price. As prices can only reflect the available information, one cannot get more profit than another. Even if you have inside information, you cannot have an edge over another investor. The stock price reflects information ranging from politics to social events, based on the investors' perception of the stock and whether this information is true. Market efficiency, therefore, means that no one can predict market prices. You cannot plan or strategize an investment to beat the market.

There are, however, irregularities that challenge efficiency. There have been investors who beat the market. Warren Buffet, for example, made billions from buying undervalued stock. Now portfolio managers and investment houses have followed suit and some have done well, while others haven't. With so many people profiting and beating the market, is it possible that you can predict the outcome of stocks? Usually, an investor who beats the market does so out of luck and not skill. A market becomes efficient when all the information is accessible and available to the investors at the same time. An investor must then have funds readily available to take advantage of this information.

The availability of information today also allows our everyday market to become effective and adjust prices. There are also laws that protect smaller companies by preventing the more powerful and successful companies from blocking a small company's entry into the market. Usually, the government gets involved and makes the markets more competitive. In some cases, the government's approval is needed before a company can raise its price. The government will examine the company's profit margin before justifying a price change.

Firms in Competitive Markets

Profit is a great motivator in any company. This is the revenue left over after all the company's costs have been paid. It is a monetary reward for shareholders or the owners of the business. Profits can be used to create incentives to cut costs and manufacture new products. Companies that are motivated by profit can spend more money on research and better technology. They become more efficient and innovative. High profit enables the company to pay better wages to their employees. Shareholders provide a source of increased income for a company, so the company needs to pay them generously. This, in turn, will enable the shareholders to release more capital into the business for future financial expansion.

Seeing that a company is under-performing or is not making enough profit to keep the business running discourages shareholders from investing in that company. They usually sell their shares which drives the price of that company's shares down, making it harder to raise funds in the future. Without profit, a company becomes unsustainable and that leads to job loss. Unprofitable firms will have to change or shut their doors. Companies must keep in mind that some products are more profitable during certain times than others. Thus, a percentage of the profit should be saved for unexpected situations, such as recession or a downturn in the economy.

Governments also charge tax on company profits, and this translates into billions each year. High profits are a great reward for entrepreneurs who start a business. If there were no profits in a business, people would be unlikely to set one up. We all need an incentive to motivate us and cash flow to keep the business afloat, and profit can be the key to both. We must, however, pursue profit in a responsible way so that we do not endanger others or cause damage to our environment. Look to start a business that has some longevity and that has steady profits. Quick money ventures can result in reckless risk-taking behavior. Any business's objective is to grow steadily from a small venture to a highly profitable larger company.

Cost of Production - The Role of Profit

There are thousands of businesses that provide a wide variety of products and services that make up our economy. These companies can be large and have thousands of employees, or they can be small, having only a few employees. Companies can have hundreds of shareholders or can be family owned and run. Any product that can be sold at a higher price makes the company more willing to produce and supply it. A company's decisions are made purely based on how they can maximize their profits.

Profit = Total Revenue - Total Cost

There could be production costs that require capital, on the other hand, there may be no charge of capital required to produce a good. There are instances when a company may choose to capitalize on an opportunity cost, which is when you lose something of value by choosing an alternative. For example, if you choose to splurge on a new car, you will have to give up a vacation to the Bahamas. In layman's terms, this means a trade-off. Most often, companies have to forego some outside opportunities when they redirect their funds to internal projects. They can lose out on earning interest on their savings, for instance, or lose an opportunity to invest in another company.

In addition, there are costs involved when the company uses funds to produce goods or services. Production costs are merely the costs involved in producing or manufacturing the goods that the company wants to sell. All companies want to maximize their profits and minimize their production costs. The reference to the quantity being produced and the materials used to create them is called the production function. Therefore, the cost to produce something can be measured using the production function method to see if they are being efficient in manufacturing goods or providing services. From the production function, you will be able to determine the profit margin between the cost of producing goods and services and selling them.

Pricing the goods is the next step, and setting the price is used as a marketing strategy. Consumers will generally only buy something if they think that the item is worth the price. If they believe that the item is of value to them, you could have a high-profit margin. However, if they perceive the item isn't worth the price, they simply will not buy it. Your company must be able to sustain itself;

therefore, the costs should not exceed your sales so that you will be able to make a profit. You can measure the costs using various methods which differ by industry and business model.

Fixed costs are costs that remain the same no matter the quantity of goods produced, and these may include rent, salaries, insurance, or interest repayments. They remain constant for a long period. Variable costs are costs that continuously change depending on the level of the production volume. These costs increase or decrease and depend on whether you make more or less of a product. The average cost is determined by the cost of producing a single unit. This is relatively easy to work out, as you can simply divide the total cost by the number of units produced to get the average cost. Lastly, you have marginal costs. This is the change in the cost to produce one additional unit of a certain product. This includes all costs that differ from the average cost of production.

Monopolies and Oligopolies

Monopolies

A monopoly is a company that is the only seller of a product and the product is one that can't be substituted. A monopoly creates barriers that do not allow other companies to compete with them. These three sources cause these barriers:

1. Resource monopoly - where a single company owns the resource. This type of monopoly is quite rare.

2. Monopolies created by the government - where the company has been given exclusive rights by the government to produce these goods. This is usually done in the interest of the public. Prominent examples include copyright and patent laws, which allow the government to create a monopoly.

3. Natural monopoly - where the cost to produce the goods by a single firm is far more efficient and can be marketed far cheaper than if many companies produced it.

A monopoly can influence the cost of production and the marketing of the product. Its revenue is maximized because the monopoly decides the quantity it will produce and the price it will charge to receive the highest profit. For the owners of the monopoly, this has a favorable outcome. However, this is detrimental to the consumer. A monopoly will always have a higher profit margin because of its power. When a customer pays the monopoly's price, the company is better off and the consumer is worse off by the same amount. The government can get involved by making these industries competitive, making them into public enterprises, or regulating their behavior. Some experts say that it would be better for the government to leave the monopolies alone. However, there have been cases where a monopoly has sold the same products to different consumers at different prices, and this will not be possible if the market is competitive.

Oligopolies

Oligopolies are two or more companies that dominate the market by producing the same type of goods. Oligopolies are usually supermarket and retail chain stores, internet service providers, etc. Even though there is no limit to the number of companies that can be part of an oligopoly, there should be enough firms that one company's decisions can influence the other companies. Usually, competition should then restrict changes in prices as customers will not purchase goods from companies with increased prices if they have an alternative. In general, groups of companies in an oligopoly are quite stable, and can both

28

compete and collaborate with each other. Thus, the companies within an oligopoly are considered interdependent on each other.

However, since oligopolies can use the price of goods to influence other companies, they are capable of some underhanded behavior. When one firm decides to drop its price, there is a possibility that the rival firms will also drop their prices, which can work against the group as a whole but may benefit an individual company. Thus, oligopolies have to be strategic in their decisions; they have to decide whether to compete with their rivals or work with them to generate a consistent pricing scheme. If they collaborate, they may raise or lower their prices in a concerted manner to generate a higher profit margin. This sets up a barrier that prevents new companies from entering the market, which can slow down progress and innovation and be detrimental to customers. Companies in an oligopoly must also choose whether they will be first to implement a new strategy, or whether they will wait to see their rival's strategy and improve upon it. Sometimes having a head start can be more advantageous if they can generate profits before anyone else; at other times, it pays to wait and then improve on the strategy.

Chapter 2:
Discover the Economic Concepts Everyone Uses, but No One Talks About

Economics, at its most basic level, is the study of human behavior. When people are faced with a lack, or too much, of something, they make decisions. These decisions can be family decisions, personnel decisions, or even business and societal decisions. Scarcity is part of life, all you have to do is look around you, and you can't miss it. Humans are always in need of some type of goods or services. There, unfortunately, is not enough to go around. Resources that are needed to produce goods and services are in short supply. Even time, of which everyone has 24 hours, is scarce.

When resources are limited, the number of goods and services we can produce also becomes limited. Now, if you pair this up with everything that humans want, you will understand why the world limited. Even the most developed countries have people who use a park bench as their beds. Not everyone has a place to live or enough food to eat. Most can't even afford healthcare. The resources required to meet these basic human needs are scarce, which leads us to believe that there is a problem with meeting the needs of others, or perhaps with meeting our own needs. Scarcity is a concept that needs to be understood first before understanding economics. Everything we consume that we don't produce by ourselves, we buy with the money we get from working for pay. Many of us never have enough because of scarcity.

In this chapter, we will take a look at the two main types of economics, microeconomics and macroeconomics. Each one will be discussed in-depth and by the end of this chapter, you will be able to distinguish between them clearly.

Microeconomics focuses on households, businesses, and workers, the individuals in the economy. Macroeconomics focuses on inflation, unemployment, and production, as well as imports and exports. Microeconomics and macroeconomics complement each other in the economy. Both perspectives are valuable and useful because they arise from different points of view. They blend together to help us understand the world of economics. Microeconomics looks at each tree, whilst macroeconomics looks at the entire forest.

Microeconomics

Micro comes from the Greek prefix, 'mikro', which means small, therefore microeconomics means small economics. This is the study of the interaction between individuals and companies and how the choices they make are best suited to the resources they have available. It has an effect on taxation levels as well as how individuals spend their money. People with limited amounts of money simply cannot buy whatever they want, nor can they do everything that they want to do. They make decisions on how to maximize their time and money. Businesses do the same, but they make decisions that will give them the best outcome in terms of profit and success in their industry.

Because these principles affect our daily lives, let's take a look at an example. How do you think this supply and demand will affect rent prices if someone is looking to rent an apartment in New York where there is high demand and a limited supply of apartments? The principles of microeconomics explain that this is the reason housing costs are so high in New York. Let's look at how it works. In order to rent the apartment, a person must settle on a budget for rent. If he/she spends too much on rent, then there won't be enough money for other expenses. Based on this information, he/she will form a budget that determines the maximum willingness to pay for the apartment. However, since apartments are in short supply, there will be others who are interested in the same apartment. They may be willing to pay more, which means he/she will have to increase the budget and cut back in other areas. This excess of demand over supply then drives up the price. This is the essence of the theory of supply and demand, which assumes that the buyers and sellers are equal.

This raises the question, what decides how much people are willing to pay? What are the factors that determine how an individual's budget should be spent? Whether they should work or not and what products and services fit their lifestyle? What determines if they will save for retirement or borrow for a current need? This depends on the theory of consumer behavior. We touched on this earlier, as this theory describes how individuals optimize the use of their limited time and money to get the maximum benefits. A similar theory applies to businesses and states that they will use their limited resources to maximize profits. In this way, microeconomics predicts how the public behaves regarding financial and economic transactions.

Yet many questions remain. How are the prices of items decided? Why are some people willing to pay more for them? How do the public's decisions influence pricing? Beyond the fundamental theory of supply and demand, microeconomics can be divided into five main sections.

The first section examines the choices and demands of the consumer. This explains how an everyday consumer, who has limited income, chooses amongst the various goods and services made available to him. Microeconomics believes that people make decisions based on satisfying their own needs and what would bring them the most happiness. This is called rational decision making, and this theory is prominent throughout the field of microeconomics.

Utility, which is also known as individual benefit, is the reason the consumer makes a decision. The consumer will be more inclined to buy a product if they feel that it is beneficial to them. Consumers determine the level of benefit given by different products, and therefore the demand for certain goods is higher than others. However, the utility of something depends on the individual's experience and current needs. Let's look at this example: We all really enjoy pizza, so eating a slice will be satisfying. However, eating the 5th slice of pizza will give you a stomach ache. With each additional slice you consume after the first one, your desire for pizza decreases. Any slice after the 5th will decrease your satisfaction and so you will choose to buy something other than pizza.

The second section of microeconomics focusses on the choices businesses make. What they should produce, in what quantity, and finally, at what price. Given that businesses want to maximize profits, they will make decisions based on market demand and their competitors. If the businesses have lots of competitors in the same market, they don't have much leeway with their pricing. Government regulations may also restrict them.

The third section combines both the consumer's choices and the company's choices. That is to say, this section looks at the decisions and interactions between consumers and companies. A customer decides when to buy a product and at what price, a business decides what it will charge for the product. Both of them make their choices based on the market price and both decide how much will be consumed and how much must be produced.

It is important to note here that the distribution of information between individuals and companies is not always symmetrical. This asymmetrical information distribution means that whoever has better information has an advantage during the transaction. For example, a used car salesman may not reveal everything there is to know about a customer's potential car purchase. On the other hand, a customer may not admit to risky behaviors when buying life insurance. This imbalance of power means the one with more information benefits, such as selling a car at a higher than reasonable price or getting insurance at a lower than appropriate price.

The fourth section of microeconomics explains the supply and demand input theory. This focuses on how companies get the resources they need to produce what customers want.

The fifth section explains welfare economics. This examines the social side of economics, such as how income and money are distributed and how this impacts the well-being of the people. It also looks at how the government may act to influence the economy and thus improve people's quality of life.

Behavioral Economics

People want different things, some want wealth and power, others want happiness and love. Each person makes economic decisions based on what they want. Consumers find themselves in situations where they do not have the option to choose a close alternative to achieve the same end. Thus, people's behavior drives the economy at a fundamental level.

Behavioral economics is the study of the effect of emotional, social, and psychological factors on individuals' economic decisions when they are uncertain. In an ideal world, we would make the best decision that would give us the most satisfaction and greatest benefit. People, when given an option, will always choose the one that they believe will maximize their satisfaction and be the best option for them. This is the rational behavior theory we mentioned earlier. However, behavioral economics says that humans are irrational and are unlikely to make clear decisions. They are easily distracted, emotional, and make decisions that are not in their best interest. Why do people choose A instead of B? Consumers would believe that they were getting a great deal if a product was introduced into the market for $800 and then reduced to $600. But what if the value of the product was $600 in the first place?

We encounter behavioral economics in nearly all aspects of our daily lives. It explains and impacts our behavior so much that we aren't even aware of it. Here are some examples:

1. Hot-Hand Fallacy - this is the belief that someone that succeeds at a random event will have great success in future attempts at that event. There is no such thing as a "hot-hand."

2. Self-handicapping - a strategy put in place where people avoid putting in effort or won't admit that they worked hard for something to protect their self-esteem.

Even though the student studied hard for a test, she tells everyone that she hardly studied for it. She has put an obstacle in her way to preemptively explain why she succeeded or failed.

3. Anchoring - influencing a person's actions by planting a thought in their minds. This is fundamental to the advertising industry.

4. Gambler's Conceit - a belief that a person can stop a dangerous course of action while they are still doing it. For example, a gambler saying that he can stop or that he'll stop when he wins.

5. Rationalized Cheating - this is when people do not think of themselves as bad people. We will more likely take a pen home than the cash equivalent. Rationalizing our actions as opposed to admitting we are stealing.

We think that we have control over our lives and the decisions we make, unfortunately, this is not always the reality. We all make use of both rational and irrational thinking. These concepts are fundamental to microeconomics, and in many ways, can be applied to macroeconomics as well, since macroeconomics as a field arises from everyone's microeconomic decisions.

Macroeconomics

Macroeconomics focuses on the entire economic process, from inflation to unemployment. What are the factors that determine how many goods and services a country needs? What determines how many jobs are available and what the standard of living should be? Why do companies expand and employ more workers and how does the economy grow? Why is macroeconomics so important?

1. Our economic system is quite complicated. Macroeconomics helps us understand how it functions.

2. It analyses and explains economic growth and how we can sustain it. It can also help to achieve a higher employment level and high economic growth.

3. It assists in stabilizing prices in businesses and advises what policies must be put in place to control inflation and deflation.

4. It finds solutions to end poverty, inflation, and unemployment.

5. It has given us a holistic view of economics and has helped us overcome the challenges of microeconomics.

Given that macroeconomics looks at the economy on a much broader scale, that of regions and nations. It looks at things like the standard of living, wealth distribution, or the purchasing power a given country or region has. One of the key measurements within macroeconomics is the output of a country, or how many goods and services are produced. This is quantified based on how much they cost and is called the gross domestic product. In general, countries want to have a high level of output per person as this means the country is prosperous and can maintain a higher standard of living.

The standard of living is measured based on the number of material goods that are available for a person, family, nation, or group. The quality of life is measured by satisfaction, relationships, and freedom. You can also relate the quality of life to the material standards. The standard of living is measured by the value of goods and services produced by everyone in the country in a year. If a country produces a lot of goods, they will be able to pay higher wages, enabling the residents to spend more. Consumer spending makes up to 68% of the US economy. When people spend money on clothing and groceries, it not only improves their lives but it also helps businesses, who in turn hire more workers. A country's residents can also benefit from a higher standard of living when the government spends money on building roads and public transport systems.

The distribution of wealth and income is the way a nation divides its wealth and income amongst the population. Wealth is the monetary value of all accumulated possessions and financial claims. Income is the net total of payments that have been received in a certain period. Income is what someone gets paid, while wealth is everything of value they've collected. Why are some countries richer than others? What can be done to address this inequality? In common terms, being rich means having more wealth and possessions than average. A country that has a higher rate of economic growth enables people to move out of poverty more quickly. People who earn a higher profit are motivated to improve production. On the other hand, people who are not rewarded are least likely to have the incentive to produce. Similarly, high productivity in a country enables quicker economic growth. This allows a country to escape poverty. Government support is needed to develop a country's economy. Nations trade with each other because they have the opportunity to benefit from each other. Thus, governments can foster trade as a way to improve their country's economy.

Purchasing power parity (PPP) is a theory used in economics that compares the living standards between countries. In order to make a comparison across nations, the production of goods and services of different categories must be included. Imported goods will sell at a higher cost than locally produced goods because of transportation costs and import duties. VAT or value-added tax can also increase prices from one country to the next. Higher prices could also be caused by deliberate action from the company to be competitive in their pricing.

Purchase power parity allows for a price comparison between countries and their different currencies. This economic term says that if there are no barriers in the trade market or no transaction costs, then the item should cost the same no matter where you are. Ideally, the shirt you buy in South Africa should cost you the same in England. Purchasing Power Parity can compare the prices of one basket of goods to another basket in a different location my measuring how to what extent factors such as taxes and poverty prevent the purchase of various goods. One mobile, one shirt, and one motorbike should cost the same in the US and in China. Every consumer in every country should have the same power to purchase goods with the right exchange rate. However, even though PPP can compare the cost of goods, it does not include the quality of goods or profits. Organizations use different baskets of goods to compute different results. Thus, price levels and inflation data are measured differently from one country to another.

Chapter 3:
Proven Principles of Economics to Be Successful and Outsmart 99% of the population

Entrepreneurs must have an understanding of economic principles to expand their businesses successfully. Even if their businesses have been successful without the full knowledge of these principles, they will find that as the business grows, problems will arise due to flaws in their processes. If unaddressed, these will grow to a point where it can seem overwhelming to the owner. Long-term business success depends on not only understanding these basic principles but also applying them to their business and marketing strategy. Understanding these principles will answer any questions you may have about your business prospects. Everything from marketing and setting prices to planning your business strategy will be covered.

First, there are five important principles that must be understood in order to analyze business decisions from an economic standpoint. Understanding these principles will allow you to determine which decisions will lead to profit and which will lead to losses for your company.

1. **Risk and return** - Small businesses are risky enterprises. Small businesses have the highest number of shutdowns and bankruptcies. On the flip side, small businesses also have the highest returns for their investors. In the past 70 years, small business stock averaged a 17.7% increase, while the large companies averaged 12.5%. Business owners must acknowledge that their business might fail and include this in their business strategy. The higher the risk that the financial asset has, the higher the return must be in order to attract investors.

2. **Marginal benefits and marginal costs** - The gains from producing an additional product are referred to as the marginal benefits, while the expenses for that extra product are the marginal costs. There is a profit when the marginal benefits are equal to or larger than the marginal cost. However, a loss will be incurred when the marginal cost surpasses the benefits. When they are equal, then the benefit has been maximized and increasing production will only increase costs. When producing a new

45

product, the marginal cost is always higher than the benefit until enough units can be sold to recoup the production costs, leading to profit. Companies should analyze the relationship between the marginal cost and the marginal benefit for each of the company's activities. If you consider increasing wages, you will have long-term employees, therefore minimizing the training of new employees. Employees that are happy give great customer service. Both of these can increase profit, but if wages are increased further, the benefits may no longer outweigh the costs.

3. **Opportunity costs** - The opportunity cost refers to the comparison between the cost and benefit of the chosen activity compared to the next best option. Small business owners must always consider the opportunity cost when they're growing their business. You have to take into account whether what you're investing in is cost-effective, without jeopardizing another aspect of the business.

4. **Sunk Costs** - These are unrecoverable expenses and should have no bearing on any future decisions once a decision has been made. These include costs such as salaries, rent, or any other expense that

must be paid whether your company has sold lots or little for the month. Fixed costs should be removed when making decisions because you will not be able to get the money for these back.

5. **Supply and demand** - Demand for goods depends on the consumers' preferences and the quantity demanded is based on the price. The quantity of the goods that are needed and their price is called demand. Supply shows how much of the goods are available in the market.

In addition to these principles, 6 essential behavioral economics principles influence the decisions made by business owners as well as customers. Economics is defined as "a social science concerned chiefly with description and analysis or the production, distribution, and consumption of goods and services" (Merriam-Webster, n.d.). Behavioral economics is founded on the observation that economists don't study humans, they study behavior. For decades, the dogma in economics has been that people are rational beings that are consistently calculating what is in their best interest, and they behave accordingly.

Now, with insights from other social sciences, behavioral economists are reshaping the subject of economics. The founder of behavioral economics, Daniel Kahneman, noted, "It seems that traditional economics and behavioral economics are describing two different species" (Kahneman, 2011). The key difference is that human beings in traditional economics are calculating, rational, and objective, but human beings in behavioral economics are emotional, biased, and unpredictable. Behavioral economics impacts all businesses, because challenges in business are challenges that humans face. Businesses must learn to understand consumers and then inspire them. The six fundamental behavioral economics principles for any business are listed below:

The Overconfidence Effect - Humans tend to overrate their performance, and they are very biased when assessing themselves. Humans cannot be objective on lots of matters. People don't exaggerate their abilities because they want to impress, they rather err on the side of self-regard. We all have something called an ego-protective cognitive mechanism. When employees were asked to rate themselves, they generally rated themselves in the top 5% of the company's employees. Over 80% of businesses believe that their customer service is excellent. However, only 8% of their customers agreed. The overconfidence effect implies that a company's brand is not aware of its shortcomings.

Temporal Discounting - Consumers make decisions based on a cost-benefit calculation, according to traditional economics. Temporal discounting is based on the fact that humans prefer to be rewarded immediately rather than wait. If we were offered $5 this month or $10 next month, we would prefer to take the first option. Rewarding customers is an attempt by companies to keep them happy. Customers are prepared to pay double for instant gratification.

Loss Aversion - Most people hate losing more than they love winning, and this describes just how the mind measures the pain of losing against the pleasure of winning. Losing a privilege is far more important than gaining it.

Anchoring and Framing - These are two powerful deviations in our minds. Anchoring is our ability to rely on the first piece of information we have. The first impression we receive determines how we interpret the information we receive after this. Salespeople use this all the time. They suggest an incredibly high price, then allow the customer to negotiate, bringing the cost down considerably. The customer will probably pay what the car is actually worth, but they feel like they got the car at a bargain price. Framing is how choice can influence the outcome. We will eat more when served on a larger dish than a smaller one. Rationally, we should only eat until we're full,

49

it shouldn't matter how big or small our plate is. The framing and anchoring principle are used to manipulate rather than inform the consumer, and this gives the company lots of power and responsibility.

Social Norms - We're all aware of the influences that society has on us; we are not immune to social and peer pressures. We all instinctively conform, and this can be used to promote positive social behavior. The need to fit in is more powerful than we think it is. Build your business on the promise of shared values and align your brand to the social norms that apply to your customers. You'll be more likely to persuade them to use your brand than another brand that fails to connect with their beliefs.

The Peak-End Rule - Humans, without even knowing it, form impressions by relying on the most intense emotional moments they experience. The peak-end rule is used as a guide by companies hoping to give customers a great experience. The customer's journey should have instances of joy throughout the process.

These insights can transform your business by changing the way you approach challenges. Behavioral economics is rooted in psychological reality. With proper research and guidance, businesses can find strategies that provide solutions to complicated problems as well as strategies that customers can relate to. In this way, they can capitalize on the power of behavioral economics.

Entrepreneurs are all about getting things done and many believe that real-life experience trumps having a degree. Even though experience doesn't always beat knowledge, some business owners have been known to pay young innovators not to get a degree. Theoretical sciences, like economics, can help people prevent many common start-up mistakes. Take a look at these five economic truths:

1. **Value is Subjective** - Entrepreneurs believe that your customers define the value of your product, not you. The value of a good or service is based on how the consumer sees it. To sell your product, you have to give the customers what they want. The cost of the product is not the main determinant of sales.

2. **Demand Curves Slope Downward** - This is also known as the "law of demand" and actually means that the higher the product's price, the fewer products are sold and vice versa. This is why price skimming works, you can target different customers, at different times, using different pricing.

3. **Price Elasticity is Relative to Demand** - Find your pricing sweet spot. This means that you need to find the ideal point between elasticity and inelasticity. Entrepreneurs know that if your price is high, you will sell fewer products. If you lower the price, you will make more money up to a point. However, if your price is very low, you will no longer be able to recover your production costs and thus lose money.

4. **One Must Consider Opportunity Costs in Terms of Both Competitors and Customers** - Customer satisfaction defines the value of your product. Opportunity cost must be considered rationally. Businesses are not only competing with each other, they're competing with the customers as well. Your product won't be sold if there are better options out there. You need to make sure that your brand stands out from the others.

5. **One Must Maximize Comparative Advantages to Create an Overall Advantage** - Do what you're good at. Comparative advantage literally means that you should do the one thing you're better at even if you're just a little better at it than something else. In any entrepreneurial start-up, talk is cheap, you should be doing

something to make ends meet. Economic truths that were relevant 250 years ago are still true today.

These insights will help you make informed decisions and have a better plan to avoid costly mistakes. Use these economic principles to guide your decision-making when determining what products or services you will produce, how you will market them, and who you wish to sell them to.

We've all heard the saying, "There's no such thing as a free lunch". In simple terms, this means that in order to get one thing, you have to give up another. Making a decision is a trade-off. Examples of this range from how someone decides how to spend their money to how a student wants to spend their time. Another example is the trade-off between efficiency and equality. The definition of efficiency is when society gets maximum benefits from scarce resources. An example of this is when the rich pay taxes and the money is given to the poor. Even though this improves equality, it also lowers the incentive for hard work. The definition of equality means a fair distribution of economic prosperity among everyone. This means that the increase in equality is at the detriment of our resources. Economics says that there is another way to look at the world and nothing is black or white. An extra $100 will make a big difference if you earn very little, however, if you earn a very high salary, you won't even notice it.

Economists have a great love for theory, sometimes to the point that they forget that theories must eventually be applied. Entrepreneurs are people of action so they can enjoy the practicalities and the fruits of economic theories. Self-interest makes the world go round. Therefore people respond to appropriate incentives as opposed to vague promises. You cannot depend on people without rewarding them. People very rarely help out without expectations of some kind of compensation. Always try and offer something in exchange for mutual gain instead of charity. Also, keep an eye on how price affects sales in your market. In higher-end markets, a lower price can decrease sales. This is called "goods with snob value" because people buying this item buy it for social status. Customers can also become loyal to a particular brand, so try to build this loyalty to secure your customer base.

While building a new business from the ground up, it's easy to forget that time is your most valuable resource. Outsource whatever you can so that you can focus on high-priority tasks. You don't have to do everything as a company or as an individual. In life, you have hundreds of opportunities to win and one chance to lose. Don't allow uncertainty to discourage you, take a risk, it may just be worth it.

Chapter 4:
The Future of
Entrepreneurship

How Can You Use These Principles to Become Successful?

A sustainable business is a firm that ensures that its business participates in eco-friendly or green activities. They make sure that whatever they do has minimal impact on the environment. A business that follows these principles will be considered green: they have committed to maintaining environmental principles in their business. They have incorporated sustainable principles when making decisions for their business, and they provide and or replace non-green products with eco-friendly ones.

Sustainability is described as a three-legged stool, people, product, profit. Sustainable businesses are forward-thinking in their approach to human rights, treating their employees well and sourcing their materials ethically. These businesses aim to meet the needs of the customer as well as the environment. Their products meet stringent green guidelines while still keeping a healthy profit margin. They aim to meet the customer's expectations without harming the earth. They make a significant effort to eliminate the harmful effects that may come from the production of their products. For example, sustainable businesses and jobs often aim to use clean energy, and in this way, contribute to reducing greenhouse gases.

The most common green initiative is going paperless, but there are many other initiatives, such as using non-toxic materials, eliminating waste, and refurbishing old pieces of furniture. The life cycle costs for the products are also taken into account because this impacts the process used to make them. There is a lot of pressure from governments, shareholders, and consumers to adopt green practices. Green investment companies are attracting much interest and can create far more opportunities to promote sustainable practices. These firms can assist small businesses with loans, business education, and networks for green products.

The origins of green businesses can be traced back to pioneering companies before WWI. Even the owner Ford Motor Company, Henry Ford, experimented with plant-based fuels. The FMC also upcycled a crate that was used as floorboards in the factory. Today Ford vehicles are made in such a way that they can run on sensible fuel.

Another company, Subaru in Lafayette, achieved a zero-landfill status and became the first vehicle manufacturer to do so. Another example is a Korean company that uses rice husks to package stereo equipment, and the husks are later recycled to make bricks. Companies are giving back on a social level as well, their employees volunteer either by giving time or through donations.

Green organizations must sustain the community, customers, and employees for them to be truly sustainable. There are numerous revenue opportunities that companies can take advantage of and some of the innovative strategies include:

1. Developing technology that allows companies to change their products and decrease waste.

2. Forming a network of like-minded companies who partner together to share knowledge.

3. Committing to integrating improved processes to reduce waste.

4. Reporting the company's performance on sustainable goals.

5. Sourcing sustainable products and having a sustainable strategy or business model.

Organizations must integrate social and ethical practices into the management system. It is no longer an option, your business must incorporate sustainability. The world is constantly changing, and having eco-friendly values can be critical to your business's long-term success. The changes in our climate and increasing income inequality are just a few of the problems that need to be addressed. Believe it or not, having a sustainable business strategy addresses both. Sustainable production of goods benefits the environment because consumers purchase those instead of goods produced in an unsustainable way. Meanwhile, sustainable and ethical sourcing of resources and pay for employees helps decrease income inequality.

Your business must be profitable so that it can do good for the environment and community. If you establish a profitable business using a sustainable model, you will be able to protect your company's brand from improper practices. Otherwise, funds spent on public relations are funds that could have been spent on the business itself. Above all, you will be protecting the environment and yourself. Sustainability should not detract your business from its goals, it should instead motivate it with a purpose and drive skilled workers and financial success. Your organization should be a place that does good and not just a place that provides a salary.

Almost everyone has become environmentally conscious and this has affected how they shop. More than 50% of US customers have changed their habits to lower their impact on the environment. Millennials are willing to pay extra for goods made from sustainable ingredients or goods that are socially responsible. There is a huge demand for sustainable products and you can get your share of it if your company commits itself to sustainable practices. Individuals that feel overwhelmed and out of their depth can collaborate with successful companies to find a solution to combat some of the world's problems. Companies that work together can solve problems that the government is struggling with. Having a sustainable strategy certainly does not mean that you have to sacrifice your profits. Quite the opposite, it has instead become crucial to the success of many companies. If your company is not sustainable, you risk losing out on profit and growth.

Recently, Samsung suspended its business dealing with a company in China because of child labor allegations. Oil companies were faced with environmental issues in countries where they operate. These are challenges many business leaders have to face in order to bring sustainability to their business. Today's business leaders are very aware that everything they do is under constant scrutiny and everything about the way the company operates is being displayed to the world via social media. They are basically running their business in a fishbowl. So how can you implement sustainability and what does this actually mean? It's about being smart in your business, not just about doing the right thing.

You must develop practical ways to apply these sustainable principles. They will, in turn, maximize your opportunities and minimize negativities. Sustainability encompasses issues such as corruption, human rights, and climate change, to name just a few. To work towards zero emissions, measures are introduced to minimize pollution and also reduce costs. To address the safety of workers, security policies are being introduced to mines and oil fields. The World Economic Forum's white paper has integrated business sustainability suggestions from experts in different areas. Therefore, it can provide a solid foundation for business leaders to incorporate and develop sustainable policies in their businesses. This resource will be invaluable to private companies, civil society groups, as well as government organizations. The white paper provides a concrete starting point and helps to frame sustainable discussions.

Recently, a large number of organizations have implemented sustainable practices voluntarily.

The quick rate at which these principles were adopted started a debate about long-term implications. Was this part of a strategic plan to promote high financial gain? Or was it to ensure that these organizations survived in the long-term? As much as it's necessary for survival, can it be enough to build a competitive advantage? Sustainability is becoming common practice and some companies have adopted this practice to improve their profit margins by exploiting cost efficiencies.

Companies can benefit from common practices because they are recognized as legitimate. Some say that sustainability is being used to generate a competitive advantage that could result in an above-average performance, i.e., doing well by doing good. However, there is a distinction between operational effectiveness and strategy. A strategy is being different by having a unique and valuable position that is difficult to match. Does this mean that sustainability can be spread through imitation, and if so, does it have a low potential for being competitive? As an increasing proportion of companies adopt sustainable practices, these practices are becoming more of a strategic necessity than a strategic differentiator. Adoption must be done earlier rather than later to make them a market leader in the industry. That said, early and effective implementation of sustainable practices has put some companies miles ahead of their competitors.

One way to help make your business sustainable is to start a home-based business. Covered below are some of the benefits of starting a home-based business that contributes to sustainability and increases your probability of success. Starting a business from home gives you a level of flexibility that you won't find if you were to rent or buy office space. Even though it requires much discipline, there can be substantial benefits. Here are a few tips for starting a winning home-based business in a weak economy.

1. The number one benefit is that you won't have to commute to the office and then back home. Your commute will be just a few steps to your home office, leaving you with more time to work on your business and decrease your carbon footprint.

2. You will have the ability to tailor your work hours and office space according to your immediate requirements. You won't have the luxury of this if you sign yourself into a lease. You can hire workers as you need them.

3. You will be able to make a tax deduction on your business income. If your business

qualifies, running it from home could be quite lucrative.

4. Having flexible work hours will allow you to work late into the night if need be. You can schedule your business hours around other obligations you have at home. With modern technology, you can communicate with customers at any time.

5. Your overheads will be relatively low as you won't have gas and phone bills, rent, or utilities to budget for. You can afford to be more generous in your pricing or if you choose to, or you can keep your prices and increase your profits.

6. You have room to test out your business to determine whether it's viable before creating overheads you may not be able to afford. Over 50% of start-up businesses fail within the first year, and if you have fixed costs, this can be a costly failure.

Any individual who creates a start-up or new business is considered an entrepreneur. He or she takes all the risks and benefits from almost all the rewards. Entrepreneurs are innovators with new ideas, products, and business procedures. They play a valuable role in the economy by using their initiative and skills. Entrepreneurs who are successful in risk-taking are rewarded with growth opportunities, high profits, and sometimes even fame. They are integral participants in the economy and offer goods and or services for profit. They face three common and challenging obstacles: overcoming bureaucracy, hiring talent, and obtaining financing. Many use their own money as funding, while others partner with someone who has access to capital. The meaning of the word "entrepreneur" comes from the French verb, *entreprendre*, which means to undertake. They are responsible for creating new things in the pursuit of profit while revealing knowledge. They break tradition and create social change. Successful entrepreneurs have all followed these five general steps:

1. Ensure Financial Stability - This is highly recommended but not an absolute requirement. Having an adequate amount of cash will ease the pressure of making quick money, giving you more time to build a business.

2. Build a Diverse Skill Set - Keep learning and trying new things. If you're building a financial company, learn the sales part of the business as well. This will be handy in tough situations.

3. Consume Content Across Multiple Channels - Read, listen to podcasts, attend

lectures, or take short courses. Familiarize yourself with what is going on in the world around you, allowing you to look at your business with new eyes.

4. Identify a Problem to Solve - Identify problems, then find a solution for them. Look at businesses as an outsider. Sometimes we're too close to see the problems.

5. Solve that Problem - Successful businesses add value to a specific problem by solving the problem.

You might have heard this being said before, "Find a way to get paid for the job you'd do for free." This is one of the most important keys to being your own boss. Interact personally with customers, you get honest feedback this way. 80% of business consists of repeated customers, so appreciate existing ones. Answer the phones personally instead of having a generic automated system. Finding the perfect fit takes time as well as trial and error so don't be afraid to tweak if needed. This is an exciting career path and the draw is being your own boss. Do enough research and make sure to include yourself in this. Have an exit strategy in the event your venture does not pan out.

Entrepreneurial economics studies the entrepreneur in the economy. It combines the human creative mind with productivity to provide profitable outcomes. Therefore, entrepreneurship should be encouraged to ensure steady growth in the economy and to develop the long-term economy. Entrepreneurs are the ones creating new industries with their innovative ventures. Economists are theory-driven and aim to model the current state of affairs, but entrepreneurs are now challenging these principles with their achievements, attitudes, and personalities. An entrepreneur is a super manager because of all the functions he performs within the firm, and he reaps the reward for his keen insight and judgment. The entrepreneur is regarded as the missing link as they invest their knowledge into production and they add value to the economy.

Bricolage is another principle that is beneficial in the entrepreneurial world. The word "bricolage" is a French word and means do it yourself. It is essential to address all new tasks immediately. Bricolage is used to explain the process of using all the tools and processes that are available at any given moment to solve the problem. It produces effective results in a world that is constantly changing. To keep a business lean is to work with what you have. Bricolage helps in bringing the focus back to the problem. Many entrepreneurs are distracted by what they would like to achieve in an ideal world. Bricolage is the idea of learning to fix problems themselves, and this idea has been around even before it had its own name. Have you ever heard someone say, "I'll do it myself"? Use bricolage to guide a conversation back to what is available and this will produce cost-effective solutions almost immediately. It is used to maintain the product and keep it constant. Bricolage has reached solutions in ways that businesses have never done before. This is because bricolage can only work with what is available within the business.

The upside of using this principle is that it brings cost-effectiveness and problem-solving to the fore as well as maximizing resources that already exist without duplicating work. There are potential downsides to this as well, bricolage focuses largely on discovery and not on creation. While focusing on only one solution, a business may miss another more lucrative opportunity. This type of thinking will probably face some kind of resistance from leadership if they feel that this is too restrictive. However, this works well with new businesses and entrepreneurs who are able to sustain the business personally. To some, preserving the business mission is key and they will not accept anything that turns their focus away from that just for the sake of practicality. Bricolage may not be the best solution in every situation, but it certainly does offer a different perspective. Keep this in your business toolbox, you never know when this will come in handy.

Chapter 5:
Applying Economic Principles to Today's World

The presence of the internet has certainly changed the way we approach the business world. Industries across the various platforms have merged technology with the traditional ways of doing business. Consumers are exposed to all kinds of virtual goods through the internet. It is estimated that 65% of young school children will have careers that don't exist today. Perhaps even in industries that don't exist yet. Entrepreneurs are also adapting to the new digital age. Digital networking has increased customer potential and has exposed businesses to new ideas through the internet. This may be the best new avenue to choose for entrepreneurs going forward.

There are multiple reasons for the growth of online entrepreneurship, and key among them is that more people can be reached, especially within millennial start-up cultures. With a constantly changing economy, many people have found that traditional jobs are less stable. With the high cost of living and more people going online, there is an abundance of opportunities and inspiration for budding entrepreneurs. It's easier than ever to know what the consumers want as you have direct contact with them. There has been a steady rise in individuals starting up their own business, and with the availability of networking websites and internet-based business models, entrepreneurs have the data they need to inspire innovation.

Entrepreneurs come from all sectors and extremely diverse backgrounds. They are starting at a younger age and are having a radical effect on the digital business world. A recent study showed that even though 95% of entrepreneurs have a Bachelor's degree, only a fraction of them have attended either business school or have any kind of formal business qualification. Entrepreneurship has never been this easy. The abundance of available online resources means that anyone can learn the skills they need to manage a business and build a network.

Not only are start-up businesses accessible, but in today's economy, the start-up business culture is far less volatile and is isolated from the downturns that affect traditional businesses. Millennials are creating jobs for themselves in a new economy instead of looking for jobs in a struggling one. With each new start-up, there are many different opportunities to succeed. As the convenience of online businesses increases, innovation within the digital world will accelerate. Advances in online platforms allow businesses and their employees to streamline their workflows. This makes more room for modern approaches and new methods for entrepreneurs.

Entrepreneurs are not only striving forward through online exposure to potential customers. They are using the cost affecting model of working remotely. The proportion of people working remotely is growing at an exponential rate. The future of new businesses and new business leaders is the digital revolution. Future entrepreneurs will be focused on operating on a global scale and engaging with online perspectives from around the world. As technological advancements spread throughout the globe, they will draw the younger, digitally-inclined generations toward digital entrepreneurship. So, what is digital entrepreneurship, and how can you get started? As digital entrepreneurship grows and as the internet becomes more accessible, this chapter will cover what you will need to embark on this new and exciting platform.

Digital Entrepreneurship

Did you know that 47% of the global population is connected to the internet and 40% of them are active on social media? What about how e-commerce has grown by 49% within the last year? Venturing online is extremely worth it! Some of the most frequently asked questions include: Is it safe? Will I be able to stand out? How do I enter this market? Let's address this common misconception first; there is no such thing as a "making money on the internet while you sleep" magic formula. You have to be willing to work hard and study the markets to ensure that you offer quality products and services to your potential clients. Here are a few tips that can help you. Starting out as a digital entrepreneur is fairly easy; all you'll need is a computer and access to the internet.

Getting Started

To set yourself apart from your competitors, you will need:

Curiosity - Show interest by asking questions. Learn as much as you can about a certain subject. Children are always asking questions. They are curious about the world around them. We need to be like them and try to get an understanding of the way something works. As adults, we simply forget to ask because we're always performing. Cultivate a curiosity about the internet. After all, you will need to understand it to found a business within it. Research is the only way you will be able to know consumer behaviors; it will show you what consumers are struggling with and thus help you find a solution that will add value to their lives.

Become Specialized - Knowledge is constantly changing, ignoring it could adversely affect what you're trying to achieve. People who study for a while and then think that they know everything miss out on valuable information. In simple terms, if you are curious but you're not too keen on studying, then digital entrepreneurship is probably not for you. That being said, you shouldn't spend hours scouring the internet for any and all information. You need to find a balance between learning and implementing this knowledge. After gaining a general foundation of knowledge, choose which niche you will specialize in. Read about your market of choice for about an hour a day and familiarize yourself with how this market operates. This will have a great positive impact on your business.

Help People - Entrepreneurship is mostly associated with identifying problems and finding solutions that have a positive impact. implementing new ideas that are innovative in ways that have never been done before. Let's take a look at Uber. What is so innovative about a taxi service? Nothing. The service they offer is not about getting people from A to B. Instead, they are innovative because their service is practical and easily accessible. Your focus should be on simple solutions with a massive positive impact, that is where your focus needs to be from now on.

Why Become a Digital Entrepreneur?

So it seems like running an online business is something you could do, but what exactly do you gain by choosing this over other start-up options? The answer is simple: freedom, cost savings, and ease of doing business. If you have access to the internet, you will be able to manage your business anywhere. You will make your schedule, meaning you can make time for what you value in life. Finally, since the internet is worldwide, scaling your business and reaching your customers becomes trivial. Let's look at each of these in a bit more detail:

Flexible Hours - When you start your business, you will be working hard and long hours to get the business off the ground. No one can be productive all the time, so working hard does not mean that you have to be working all day long. By defining your schedule, you will become more efficient. You can be flexible in your work hours to spend time with family or allow for unforeseen circumstances.

Cost Savings - Your start-up costs will be at a minimum. By working from home, you save on rent, utilities, and even taxes. The space you occupy will vary according to your business needs but is typically significantly less expensive for digital businesses than traditional brick-and-mortar stores.

Easy Access to Your Target Market - More than 50% of the world's population uses the internet. Starting an online business is the way to go to reach more people. A physical store has mobility and geographical limitations, while digital businesses can reach the world. By targeting your advertisements, you can make sure that you reach your customers, no matter where they live.

Easily Scalable - You can scale your business by increasing production and sales without increasing your marginal costs. This does depend on your personalized business model, but ultimately it will be easier to scale a digital business than a physical one. For example, if you choose to design online courses, you will never run out of stock, and anyone who pays for it will be able to access it immediately. With a physical classroom, you have to pay to rent space, to furnish a classroom, to print materials, and you must go where the students are.

What Can You Do as a Digital Entrepreneur?

The next step will be to decide exactly what you'd like to do as an entrepreneur. Your creativity really only limits potential answers, but here are some of the most common options:

Producer - These are individuals who develop content that can be used online. The content can come in various formats, like podcasts, online courses, e-books, etc. All you would need to become a producer is useful knowledge that you would like to share with others.

Affiliate - These are professionals who promote 3rd party goods for commission. This is a great business option for those who don't want to create their own content but who already have online influence.

E-commerce - This type of commerce is where products are sold online and delivered to the customer's home. This business model has changed the way people buy goods and has been steadily increasing in popularity.

Technological Solutions - Start-ups are businesses that are birthed online but can migrate to the physical world if needed. Once again, you must identify a problem that the consumers are faced with and find a simple, easy to understand solution for this.

Digital Influencer - There is no limit to digital influencers, and they often don't have a niche. It is commonly known as the profession of the moment. An example of this is a blog or YouTube channel about make-up. Brands that want to reach your audience will want to create a partnership, often through sponsorships. Influencers can also run ads or use affiliate links to make money, essentially more views and clicks make you more money.

How to Build Your Business

You've now decided what you want to do, but what are the concrete steps you should follow to get started? Some of the best and worst lessons are learned through experience, and although no amount of preparation can prepare you for everything, there are steps that you can take to make sure your business does not end before it gets off the ground.

Identify Your Strengths - What are your strengths? If you're not too sure, try the SWOT method: Strengths, Weaknesses, Opportunities, Threats. This is very easy and simple for you to use as a guide. Use this like you would a pros and cons list. Divide a page into four columns, and then each column into two, essentially having two columns for each heading. Under each heading, write down the positive impact and the negative impacts for your business. This may seem like a tiresome exercise, but by the end, you will have a much better idea of where in the market you are most likely to succeed.

Choose What Type of Product You Would Like to Offer - Now that you know what you are good at, you can find the perfect niche. A niche is a specific market segment, such as the birthday cake segment of the baking industry. Choose something you have a bit of knowledge in and something that you enjoy doing. This way, you can capitalize on the strengths you identified earlier to become an expert. For example, you may have a hobby that you are skilled at and enjoy teaching to your friends. If you base your business around this, then you will likely find the process quite intuitive and enjoyable. The most important question of all is, if you had a choice, what would you like to do for the rest of your life?

Next, find out if there is a demand for what you are offering. Would you be able to make a comfortable living from this? Do a bit of research to see what the demand is for what you're offering. Be aware of what is trending. Just like how we change the way we dress depending on the season, many trends are transient and will fade with time. So you will need to keep a keen eye on market shifts and be prepared to adapt if you choose to pursue something just because it is a current trend.

Otherwise, focusing on something with a constant level of demand can give your business more stability and may be preferable as you're just starting out.

Analyze the Market as Well as Your Competitors - Get to know your competition and know them well. This helps you gain some insight as to how they operate and how you can find a competitive edge. Visit your competitors' sites or other similar sites, and focus on what's relevant to your target market. Take note of how they interact with their customers and what they communicate to them. Remember, you are gathering information only. You don't want your business to be a carbon copy of another. Ideally, you would like to improve upon the template they provide so that your business stands out.

Create a Financial Plan - An online business is cheaper than a physical one, but you will need to save up or otherwise acquire some capital before starting up. Get a handle on your personal finances, such as how much you spend in a month, and build up savings in case your business is not profitable right away. Have a detailed plan for what costs will be associated with the materials or equipment you will need, with designing your online platform, with advertising your goods, and with the day to day running of your business such as paying employees or utility costs. Determine what financial targets you will need to hit in order to break even, and anything you make beyond that will be your profits. This information will then be used to determine your sales targets based on the price of your goods.

Get a Domain - If you are creating content or a virtual store, this should be the first step. Choose a domain name that will accurately represent your business. Keep it short and easy to remember so that potential customers can find your page. Visit register.com or godaddy.com to see if your business name has already been chosen. If your product is digital, you don't necessarily need to buy a domain as there are online platforms that you can use to advertise your product.

Make a Prototype of Your Idea - To know whether your idea is feasible, ask yourself these questions: What problem does your product solve? Is it easy to understand? Will it be better than your competitors' products? Would you be willing to buy your product?

Review your plan if you answered "no" to any of these questions and find ways to improve your plans. You should be able to make the necessary improvements to give you a higher chance of success when your product is ready to be launched.

Promote Your Business - It is time to promote your product. Have a good strategy to start advertising your product and to deliver it to your customers. Show them the value of what you are offering. The right audience will pay for it. Soon there will be more than 2.7 billion people using social media. However, not all of them will be part of your target audience. Your communication should be directed towards those who are likely to be interested in your products, and even though you can reach more people, try not to. No matter which platform you choose to use, make your content specifically for that platform.

There are many ways you can reach potential customers. Having an email list is an invaluable asset to any business owner. Make sure you create one of your own instead of purchasing one. Advertising is another great way to impact potential customers; just ensure you have good quality images and great content. Advertise on multiple networks to increase your product visibility. You may also benefit from having your own social media pages, where you create quality content and answer questions honestly. This will help potential customers become comfortable enough to start buying your product. Great content quality will bring lasting results as this builds relationships between you and the customer. Not all marketing types are optimal for every niche, so experiment a bit and find out what works for you.

<u>A Short message from the Author:</u>

Hey, are you enjoying the book? I'd love to hear your thoughts!

Many readers do not know how hard reviews are to come by, and how much they help an author.

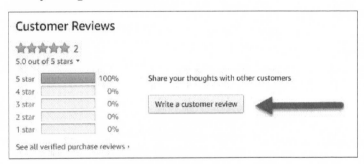

I would be incredibly thankful if you could take just 60 seconds to write a brief review on Amazon, even if it's just a few sentences!

Thank you for taking the time to share your thoughts!

Chapter 6:
The Secret to Earning Income with Recycled and Upcycled Materials

Businesses of any size can make a difference for the environment, and there's nothing wrong with making a little money on the side while doing this. This chapter will give you practical advice to realize your dream of starting an ethical business. There are many ethical businesses you could start, and we will talk about a few more in later chapters, but for now, we will look at how you can base a business around recycled and upcycled materials.

Did you know that you can make ends meet by repurposing used clothes, newspapers, plastic, etc.? Many people have learned how to turn recycled trash into a thriving sustainable business. This has become a global mega-trend as over 90% of the world's customers want eco-friendly or environmentally friendly products. Eco-friendly items have seen an increase in sales each year, and sustainable fashion has increased by 75%. This not only helps save the planet, but it is also extremely profitable. Consumers are willing to pay more for repurposed, eco-friendly items. You can turn your concern for the environment into ideas that will fill your wallet. Learn about the thousands of craft ideas that use recycled materials, how to stand out on social media, and how to promote your business on all social media platforms and craft markets.

Curbside collection has supplied a tremendous amount of recycled materials, from paper to glass, and recycling has become an economic system all of its own. The collection of these recyclables outweighs their market value. As the demand for recycled materials grows, it has turned into a competitive advantage for farsighted businesses. With the regulations governing environmental issues becoming tighter, companies have strategically formed alliances with community groups and public organizations. Managers of some of the world's high profile companies such as Coca-Cola and American Airlines have invested in repurposed products and have found that it's in their best interest to do so. They have increased their profits and cut down on waste products. The value of recycling is long-term and makes perfect economic sense.

With everyone jumping onto the green bandwagon, certain misconceptions must be dispelled, such as recycled products being of poor quality and costing more. Businesses that are becoming sustainable by adapting to the new eco-friendly market are providing solutions to their customers. A report by the Retail Industry Leaders Association (RILA) estimated that 68 million Americans would spend at least 20% more on eco-friendly products, and base this on their personal values regarding the environment. Another survey concluded that 87% of US millennial social media users would pay more for sustainable products. Technology has also played its part in providing forward-thinking green initiatives by cloud-based storage and barcode scanners.

The newest trend in sustainability is upcycling, the reusing of materials and objects that have been discarded. Products of a higher quality and value can be created using textile waste. Yarns and materials created by using plastic bottles have become an eco-centric trend. These materials are used to make clothing and accessories. High profile fashion houses are also getting involved. Tommy Hilfiger has launched a line of 100% recycled cotton jeans in 2019, and Adidas has made 6 million pairs of shoes by upcycling plastic collected from the ocean. Sustainability and upcycling in the retail industry are here to stay. Retailers and brand houses need to be innovative to remain relevant to a growing eco-conscious market.

ycling, in layman's terms, really means taking something that is slightly dated and making it better by either fixing it or changing it. So, what can you upcycle? Well, anything! Start by painting an old antique replica or even an old chair. A fresh coat of paint can take a tired old piece of furniture and turn it into something new and exciting. Any item that needs a bit of fixing up can be refreshed with your DIY tools. Upcycling is quick and easy, especially with all the products available on the market for these tasks. The transformation of a product from tattered to valuable is more appreciated when it has a rags to riches story behind it. This opens up another avenue for marketing recycled and upcycled goods. Transforming an old airbag into a backpack, or a mosquito net into a sleeve for a laptop, creates what is known as a product biography and gives the product a brand new identity. Recycling is commonly practiced, but now upcycling is becoming more popular and is in such demand that even established companies incorporate it into their business strategy. The psychology behind this is that the customer feels special when a product has a storytelling ability. Value is generated from what would otherwise be considered a waste product, by reshaping and prolonging its life.

As much as there are similarities between recycling and upcycling, there are also differences. Recycling is the breaking down of old materials into raw materials before they can be transformed and repurposed. Upcycling takes an old or outdated item and transforms it by giving it a new identity.

The Skills You'll Need to Sell Products Online.

Now that you've got some ideas of what you can craft out of recycled items or what you might upcycle, you'll need to know how to sell your products. There are plenty of resources available online that you can use to sell your products, and we'll get into the specifics in the next section. First, let's go over the skills and beneficial habits you'll need to develop to become a successful online entrepreneur. It seems obvious, but you must be comfortable online and on the internet, love what you do, and practice to hone your skills. Keep a record or document the steps you've taken so that you can repeat them at a later stage. Know your target market and display your work on as many sites as you can to get more views. Invest in a good camera to ensure that your photos are a good representation of your products. Have excellent customer service and fair pricing. The demand for well made and cleverly designed products has increased dramatically over the last few years, and consumers are looking for one of a kind items as opposed to something mass-produced. To be successful, you need to combine your talent and intuition and then commit yourself to become a professional.

This chapter will be your guide to getting your online business off the ground. You will learn how to promote your craft and sell yourself as a crafter. You will be able to establish your very own website and set up a business system that will propel you into success. Everyone wants to be their own boss and to make millions doing what they love, but before you can embark on the amazing journey, ask yourself if this is right for you. Do you have the right traits to establish and run a successful online store? Entrepreneurs are creative thinkers; they are ready to solve problems, find new opportunities, and take advantage of what's available. Ask yourself the following questions:

1. Can I research my competition and their work and make adjustments to mine to create a better product?

2. Will my creations be popular with the customers, and will I enjoy my hobby as a job?

3. Do I have the time and money to spend to get this business up and running?

4. How much capital do I have to sustain myself in the start-up phase?

5. Will my prices be competitive enough to generate a customer base and income?

Online businesses are generally a one-man show, so you will need to do all the tasks required to run your business and to make it a success. You have to be organized and focused, motivated and productive, market your products and make them better if needed. You need to have a quick response time because customers have no way to interact with you apart from the messages on your site. Respond to questions and queries within 24 hours. Be polite and courteous in your responses and acknowledge messages even when you don't have an immediate answer. Keep the communication going, from the initial query to the order that has been sent out. Your customers will determine the kind of service that is expected of you. Listen to them and take note of everything they say, from thank you to criticism.

The Steps to Start Selling Online

Hobbypreneurs are people who've turned their hobby into a successful business by marketing themselves on a global platform such as Etsy. This has become a simple and popular way of generating an income from your hobby. Most people want to know which hobby can make you money, and the answer is: your hobby. All you need is some creative thinking and good business sense and you could be on your way. Anything sells, from knitting beanies to woodwork, from jewelry-making to kitchenware, there are endless possibilities. Put a price tag on your hobby. However, if your hobby is skateboarding, it would be difficult to skateboard daily and see your bank balance increase. You need to audit your hobbies to see which one has the greatest potential to make money. Don't count anything out; sometimes the least likely hobbies will have the highest money-making potential. Do some research, and remember that it is very likely that someone else is selling a similar product, so compare pricing and see what the best-sellers are. Most online stores are saturated with similar products, so you need to find a way to set yours apart. Hobbies are supposed to be fun, so if you're no longer having fun, it's no longer a hobby.

Figure out where to source the products you would like to sell. Try contacting those in your community, as using local materials can have a great positive impact on both your surroundings and business. Selling online can seem quite daunting at first. It's fairly easy to set up, so don't worry about it being too costly or taking too long. Have a plan for selling, either through a marketplace, on social media, or your very own store. Once you have the products you will sell, you need to attract the customers. There are many ways to sell to an online market. The four most common ways are listed below, and the great thing is that you don't have to choose one or the other. You can use them all.

1. **E-commerce stores:** This allows you to integrate your online store with social media or marketplace. You can use the apps provided by Facebook, Amazon, etc., to link your store in such a way that you can sync your products, so whoever visits your Facebook page will see the products that you have on your online store. It is very easy to manage, and you can update your business and all social media platforms so they are updated automatically as well. You can manage your business with your smartphone from anywhere at any time. You are always in control of how your online store looks and feels, and you can control your products' presentation. You can make changes that you feel are necessary without waiting for Facebook or Amazon. Your sales can be processed quickly and your products can be showcased faster than before, leaving you to focus on the more important parts of your business. You are able to literally run a 24-hour store. The top three e-commerce platforms are:

   a. Shopify

b. Wix

c. BigCommerce

Your store can be successful no matter which platform you choose to use. They are all designed to promote your product. You first need to create an account before you can start selling. Use the free trial period to test out the platform before committing to it and paying the monthly fee to use it. Building your own online store makes you look like a professional, which makes you a credible seller. You must build trust in the online shopping community for them to buy from you. E-commerce platforms have two excellent reasons for you to use them to sell online: abandoned cart recovery and mobile responsiveness. The abandoned cart recovery allows you to contact customers who have not yet confirmed their order for whatever reason, giving you another chance to close the sale. Over 39% of online shoppers use their mobile phones to place an order in an average month. Your store must work well on a mobile as well as a desktop. E-commerce platforms are automatically designed to work on mobile. So, no matter how big the screen is, buying your products will run smoothly. E-commerce platforms can be compared to a Swiss army knife, where you have lots of tools easily and readily available from one platform.

2. **WordPress:** They started out as a blog publishing system. In the last few years, they've begun to support web content and have become one of the most popular platforms in the content solutions industry. This is a great option for an online store. Here are some easy steps to get started with WordPress: Choose a product that you would like to sell and decide on what the niche will be, digital or physical products. Buy a domain name which, in simple terms, means a URL and add an extension, typically .com or .net. Make sure that it is easy to remember and easy to say. Keep in mind that non-profit organizations use the extension .org. Keep the domain name short. Use acronyms if your name is long because your site will gain popularity more quickly if the domain is easy to remember.

The next step is to obtain a host for your site. Luckily, WordPress offers hosting packages, making it very convenient since everything is available in one place. Note that if you plan to set up your site elsewhere, make sure that you sign up with a reputable host with great customer service. When you are one hundred percent sure of your choice, sign yourself up.

Once you've downloaded WordPress onto your site, you will have a walkthrough guide to get you through all the technical stuff. Now that you have your WordPress site set up and your products are all lined up, it's time to start selling. Choose an e-commerce platform. Now it's time to make sure that the site is working the way it should. Go through the processes as a customer to ensure that any problems are ironed out before going live. Check that all the digital files have been uploaded correctly, you may also want to check the download speed. Don't forget about your emails. See if the wording and branding are correct before you start advertising.

3. **Marketplaces:** Selling on marketplaces such as Amazon, Etsy, and eBay is great for people who want to sell their product quickly and don't mind competing with millions of other people. Amazon has over two million sellers and is extremely popular. For you to sell on these marketplaces, all you need to do is create an account and list the products you wish to sell, along with the price and description. Accept payment and ship the goods. It's that easy. You can enter the marketplace quite easily as there is little to no barrier to entry. Etsy and Amazon have a

huge number of customers that will ensure that you can immediately start selling. The trick though, is for you to stand out from the crowd of other sellers. You cannot rely on the marketplace to promote your product. In fact, Amazon searches are constantly changing, so your product will be visible one day but not the next. You must have a unique brand that allows you to stand out so that you're not one of many sellers promoting the same product. There will almost always be someone new on the market with a lower price that will take the customer away from you. A trustworthy brand can be a valuable asset in the long-term. Marketplaces do charge a fee, so read the fine print before you commit.

By selling on Amazon, you are using their reputation to sell your goods. Everything from DVDs to electronics is sold on this platform. Amazon is so popular that you may find yourself in competition with Costco or Walmart. Amazon's fees are based on what you're selling as well as the quantities sold. For a little bit extra, they will provide you with a delivery service.

Etsy is a platform used mainly by artists and crafters and thus can be a great choice for sustainable crafts. The customers are more focused on a specific type of product. Buyers and sellers are like-minded, so they don't mind spending a bit more on an item. Etsy also charges a fee, so remember to check it out before signing up.

You can sell almost anything and everything on eBay, therefore it's almost impossible to build a business here. Because eBay is structured on a bidding model, customers are not obligated to pay you until the time runs out, and until then you will not be sure how much money you will receive. Also, check out their fees, eBay charges 10% of what you've sold.

4. **Social media sites:** With over two billion users, Facebook is currently the biggest social media site in the world, and you can use this platform to match your product to the consumer easily. Before you can get started, you must create a business page. Facebook is a bustling platform, so don't expect a response by just posting your product. Find a way to hold the customers' attention. Run promotions and give out discounts, ask questions, and use videos and jokes if you have to. Don't undersell your page, post regularly to get enough traffic through your page to make it stand out. Link your Facebook page to an e-commerce

platform and you will be able to manage your inventory and products in one place. If you choose to sell exclusively via Facebook, this can be quite time-consuming as all orders will have to be handled manually.

Now that you know which platform you will be using, putting together a business strategy is the next step. Getting an online business off the ground can be a bit tricky and seem daunting. Most of these we touched on before, but make sure you have answers to the following questions:

1. How many products must I sell to make a profit and how will I achieve this?

2. What would it cost to buy or produce an item and have it delivered to the customer?

3. Keep it simple and do some research on your competitors. After all, you're learning as you go. Who are your competitors?

4. What are consumers spending their money on and can I match their needs to my products?

5. Will potential customers be able to find my products online?

Having the right customer for your products is critical to success, so you need to supply products that someone needs. To determine what products are most likely to sell, take a look at what the most successful companies are advertising. Provide products for the market and don't look for a market for a product. It does not matter how good your online store looks, or how professionally you handle business, you are not going to sell if no one's interested in what you are selling. Ensure that there is a demand for your product. Since you will be selling your own creations, much of the draw lies in the personal touch.

So, what will sell online? Wouldn't it be nice to know what products will be trending in the next few months? If there was a way to do this, we'd all be multi-millionaires. One thing that you can do now that you have a product in mind is a google trend search. This is a great tool that will enable you to see what's trending and what's not. Search a few options and take a look at the most popular and trending product results. This will give you a heads up on what to offer your customers. If you take note of the spikes, you will also see when the best time would be to increase your sales.

Online forums are also a great way to find out what customers are thinking about. Reading online forums can be like having a million or so customers telling you what they think and what can be changed in a product. The key though, is to sell what you love and what you are passionate about. It will be easier to sell something you enjoy. However, don't overlook the money-making potential of another product. The next step would be for you to source the raw materials at a reasonable price. Contact wholesalers or retailers and find out if you can put your brand on them, especially if you will be bulk buying and storing. You can also look for individuals in your local community who may be willing to work with you, such as contractors who may have scrap wood or plastic waste you can repurpose.

Chapter 7:
The Complete Guide to Producing Your Own Food for Profit

You've probably heard or read about the bio-integrated system of aquaponics. This chapter will cover the basics of this process. The combination of two different main elements, fish farming and plants growing in a water source, is the basis of aquaponics. The interaction between the two provides benefits for both to thrive. The fish waste in the water provides the plants with the nutrients they need for healthy growth. The plants use the nitrogen from the water and this, in turn, purifies the water for the fish. This creates a self-sustaining system that generates plant and animal produce. Aquaponics reduces problems that aquaculture and hydroponics have when used alone. Growing huge quantities of fish place a strain on the water they're being grown in. The water becomes polluted with chemicals and waste from the fish, necessitating constant maintenance. Plants grown hydroponically need fertilizer to grow because the water does not have enough nutrients to sustain them. This is how aquaponics works to overcome these challenges:

1. The fish enrich the water with their excrement.

2. The bio-filter circulates the water.

3. The plants grow quite quickly as a result of the nitrates in the water.

4. The water that goes back into the fish tank is pure and oxygenated.

This cycle benefits both the fish and the plants. However, we have yet to mention the third and most important part of this system: microorganisms. These microorganisms make the nitrogen cycle possible and more efficient. To have a successful aquaponic system, you need to use nitrifying bacteria because a mechanical filtration system can't filter out all the ammonia from the water. Biofilters get rid of decaying matter that has dissolved in the water through physical filtration. The microorganisms within the filter then convert the excess ammonia and nitrite to nitrate, which the plants use to grow happily.

Can you imagine being able to grow your own food? You can raise your own fish and grow your favorite vegetables, and there's very little work involved. Aquaponics systems are becoming quite popular and almost everyone wants one.

Professional and pre-made aquaponics systems can be costly to buy. Therefore many have resorted to building their own. There are loads of really diverse systems from the simple DIY to the more professional hi-tech systems. There are considerable benefits to having a system like this in your home. Here are a few of them:

1. Aquaponics husbandry eliminates weeds and tiny insects from your garden.

2. The nutrients in the water are continually being circulated, so none of the nutrient-rich water is lost.

3. Aquaponics conserves water by using about 1/10th of the water required by other systems. This is a great advantage in areas where there is a shortage of water.

4. The ecosystem is natural, so no harmful chemicals or pesticides will be used.

5. The system is space-efficient so you can place it anywhere and in any room inside or outside your home.

6. This system can be scaled to your requirements.

7. You can get fresh, nutritious food that's free from toxic chemicals.

Even though aquaponics is a very simple system, you do need some know-how if you plan on making one. Here is a list of equipment you will need to make a simple aquaponics system:

Tools:

- A drill
- Drill bits: 3/16", ½" and ⅞."
- A hacksaw
- A pipe cutter
- Razorblade
- Cutters
- Thread seal tape

Materials:

- 15-gallon plastic grow bed
- ½" irrigation tubing
- 2 ½" ball valves
- 3 ½" barb adapter
- ½" flex pipe tee insert
- ½" MNPT X barb 90-degree elbow
- 2 x #14 O-rings
- 2" PVC pipe 8 ¾" long
- 2" PVC cap

- 1 ¼" PVC pipe 6 ⅝" long
- 1 ¼" PVC cap
- ½" PVC pipe 5 ⅝" long
- ½" male adapter
- ½" female adapter
- 2 ½" PVC pipe 3" long
- 2 ½" 90-degree elbows
- Hydroponic rock and pea gravel combination
- 30-gallon plastic fish tank
- Black plastic sheeting
- Plastic storage shelves
- 100 - 130 GPH submersible pump

How to build the automatic siphon:

1. Insert the ½" pipe into the ½" male adapter.

2. Drill a hole at the bottom of the grow bed and pass this through the hole with an O-ring. This will ensure that there are no leaks from the grow bed.

3. Attach the male adapter from the outside to the female adapter.

4. The two 90-degree elbows and the 3" PVC pipe are then inserted into the adapter, making up the drainage assembly.

How to build the water pump system:

1. Secure the pump to a paving stone using a zip tie.

2. Using a barbed tee fitting, run the ½" irrigation tubing from the motor.

3. Attach a piece of irrigation tubing and threaded adapter to this and screw in a ball valve.

4. Attach a longer piece of irrigation tubing to the other barb, then attach a threaded adapter, a ball valve, and another threaded adapter.

5. Add more irrigation tubing and the 90-degree elbow fitting. The ball valve will control the water flow.

How to test the system:

1. Place the system in its designated area and fill your tank with water.

2. Secure the water inlet for the grow bed. Carefully plug in the water pump as per the directions it came with.

3. Adjust the ball valve to get the flow of water you need.

4. Ensure that there are no leaks and make corrections if needed.

Stock and testing your system:

1. Add seedlings of your choosing to the grow bed.

2. Add a few fish to the tank.

3. Test the water twice a day, morning and evening, using an aquarium kit.

4. Test the pH levels and keep a log. Record the results and the quality of the water.

5. Now that you're up and running, all that's left to do is to feed the fish and get ready to harvest your vegetables.

Starting a Business Using Aquaponics

This type of agriculture has been around for a while now. There is a global demand for the aquaponics market. Many people are attracted to it because it presents a solution to the problems society faces in terms of food production and quality. Organic food is in high demand these days, and because the population is increasing and farmland is in short supply, aquaponics is becoming very profitable. Aquaponics is sustainable and eco-friendly and has made producing food efficient and low-cost. Aquaponics is not only for the backyard gardener, but it is being used for commercial purposes to meet the demand for organic food.

Starting up a commercial aquaponics system can be challenging. However, because of its efficiency and low-cost maintenance, it can turn out to be very profitable. Fresh, organic food is harvested much quicker than traditional farming methods; therefore, aquaponics is a worthwhile investment. Like any other business venture, careful planning, a strong business plan, and a committed team are essential to building your business. Before starting your business, you need to consider your main reasons for starting a commercial aquaponic business. Focus on your business plan, get expert advice, and identify resources that will help develop your business. Also, look out for issues that may hinder the progress of your business. Ask yourself these questions: What are the experiences that will help me with the farming operations? Will this business be for-profit and income? Do I have a location to run this from? What are the environmental issues that may crop up? Who on my team can help with business and financial strategies?

Your business plan should look something like this:

<u>Overview of your business:</u> Have a vision statement, a mission statement, and the goals for

your business.

Vision: State the purpose of the business plan and prove you have an understanding of what is contained in the plan. Describe your vision for the commercial aquaponics farm and how it will tie into your personal beliefs and values. It should answer questions on community and environmental issues as well as how the farm will benefit the community.

Mission: These principles will guide you to the goal of your commercial aquaponics farm. It should also state the purpose and expectations of the farm and its customers.

Goals: Set short-term and long-term goals for the farm. Focus on the start-up process and extend your goals forward in time to what you would like the farm to achieve in the long-term.

Management and Organization: Set out the management and organization structure of the commercial aquaponics farm. How will the farm be managed and organized? Register your farm according to the legal requirements of the business; non-profit, sole proprietorship, or corporation. You may need to check the local and state requirements. Carefully set out the management team structure, including who will manage and run the farm, what will their skills and responsibilities be, how will managers and board members be paid, how will the farm be managed and run?

<u>Marketing Strategy:</u> Identify your products and marketing strategies. The most important part of a business plan is to have a specific strategy for the sales and marketing of your product. Understanding the market is key, who are your potential customers and competitors? You have to believe in your product to convince potential investors that this is a viable market. Your business plan should include an introduction to your commercial aquaponics farm. These products will be produced and then sold, as well as how you plan on distributing the products, making them available to the consumers.

Identify your target market and their purchasing and spending rate. Gain an understanding of the location where your farm will be situated, will inflation or the employment rate affect you? What are the cultural and social factors that will affect your farm? Take into consideration your customers' values and behaviors. Do they have a preference for a specific crop? Ensure that your produce is readily available to the consumers so that they are more likely to buy from you. Ensure that the product meets the consumer's expectations by handling the crops with care from the time they've harvested to the time they are on the shelves. How will you be storing the product before distribution to ensure that the produce is fresh and of good quality?

With this information on hand, market your product as unique and different from the competitor's product. Note that your pricing must be comparable to your competitors. Take into consideration how you will dispose of products that are not sold. Identify your competitors and consider how you plan on competing with them. List your commercial aquaponic farm's advantages over the competitors as well as the disadvantages. Include what they offer to the market, their pricing, and how established they are in the area.

Operating Strategy: After you've identified the type of products and the quantity you would like to produce, prepare your operating strategy. List the methods you plan to use, such as the raft system, a nutrient film-based system, or a media-based system. What approach will you be using to raise the fish and plants? Prepare and discuss a schedule from the initial planting to the harvesting of the product. What are the volumes of fish and plants that must be managed when they're harvested? Do you plan on selling the fish as a product of the farm, or will they be used only to provide nutrition to the plants? Do you plan on planting and harvesting throughout the year or will it be seasonal?

The plants and the fish are dependent on each other, so ensure that you have enough fish to provide adequate nutrition for the plants. Invest in a cycling system that will need the needs of your farm. You will need a plan to manage the water pH, temperatures, nitrates, and ammonia levels. A good monitoring system will be needed as this is very important when growing healthy fish and plants. When choosing these systems, you will need to know the size of the system you plan to have and the capacity of fish and plants it will hold. Approximate the amount of fish and plants that you plan on producing and what the estimates would be for about five years. Discuss repeated production and how you will make sure this is consistent for each of these years.

List the resources that you will need, such as equipment, land, buildings, and anything necessary to start your commercial aquaponics farm. Also include waste disposal and the water and electricity requirements to meet the needs of your farm. What are the other objectives that you aim to meet, and how will this impact the environment? Where will the farm be situated for the next five years, in your home, a building, or a greenhouse? Most often, commercial aquaponic farms are in a controlled environment. Do you intend to buy or lease the property? What additional equipment and supplies such as tools, vehicles, tanks, etc., will be needed for the next five years, and how will you acquire them? Don't forget about a communications system, for monitoring the system remotely as well as internet and phone lines. Before you start your commercial aquaponics farm, make sure that all the environmental assessments have been done on the property and that all known issues have been resolved.

<u>Human Resources:</u> Estimate the number of workers that will be needed to manage and operate the business in the first five years. Identify the number of daily tasks and the workers that will complete them and include management, administrative as well as farm laborers. Create positions and the number of workers that you will need for each position. How many will be full-time employees and how many will be hired on a part-time basis? Do you plan on engaging volunteers to work on the farm? Do you plan on having a training program for the staff? How will you pay the staff and what would you estimate the salaries for each position to be? How would you structure the working hours? Will you have benefits such as medical coverage? Will you be using a monitoring system to reduce labor or hiring additional workers for harvesting? Ensure that you have all the necessary licenses and permits required to start your commercial aquaponics farm. You must

consider the governmental regulations, planning, zoning, and building requirements set out by the state in which you plan on operating.

Financial Strategy: Estimate the expenses that will be needed to start your commercial aquaponics farm. Draw up a five-year projection and include all expenses like marketing, operating, and human resources. This should also include preparations, administrative, and start-up costs. What is your income prediction annually for the first five years? The income must include sales projections as well as any losses from unsellable products. Also, include any donations or other monetary resources expected. Include current fixed assets such as buildings, furniture, machinery, etc., and any assets you may purchase in the future. List all the potential sources of funding, how much you will need, and how you intend to get the funding. The funds should have an impact on the business plan, ensuring that you achieve your goal of starting your very own commercial aquaponics farm.

There will, however, be potential risks that need to be considered. There will be risks in production as there may be crop failures, there will be risks in marketing, and your competitors may reduce their prices. You need to identify these potential risks and minimize them as they will definitely have an impact on the success of your business plan. To run a successful commercial aquaponics business, you need to have some kind of business experience in this field, or you will have to hire someone who does. Good business understanding, knowledge, and experience can guarantee you success in your business, while focusing on profitability and the idea of a commercial aquaponics farm does not.

Invest in yourself by educating and training yourself. Gaining knowledge in how aquaponics works and the science behind it is paramount to a thriving business. Speak to other successful aquaponics farmers to learn how they operate their business. Have a look at their facilities to see how their daily operations run. The right advice from the right people is important for your farm's success.

Do your research on pricing so that you can be competitive. Be knowledgeable about market trends so that you know which products are in demand. It is always better to start small and then build your business up from there. You will be able to gain some knowledge of how the business works, because no matter how much research you do, you will only truly understand how the business works from experience. You will be able to adapt quickly with a smaller and more manageable aquaponics farm. Things can suddenly go wrong, and you will be able to fix the problems easily and more efficiently. Even though aquaponics has the potential of making a lot of money, it is not easy work. You have to have a love for it to enjoy this challenging and labor-intensive field. Approach this business with the right mindset, extensive planning, and knowledge, and you will be able to achieve a successful and profitable commercial aquaponics farm.

Chapter 8:
The Ultimate Slow Fashion Guide for Anyone

Sustainability is not only about the planet, it's also about people and profit. Sustainable fashion is a circular system where clothes, shoes, and accessories are produced with integrity. Where laborers are treated humanely, the earth's resources are taken into consideration, and brands don't have to cut corners to be successful. Products are designed to be versatile and durable. Making fashion sustainable is extremely important, as fashion is the second most polluting industry. Over 150 billion items of clothing are produced each year.

Sustainable Fashion, to Purchase or Upcycle?

Even though over 70% of consumers say that sustainable fashion is very important to them, the fashion industry's efforts are slowing down. The fashion industry's interest varies, while some are conscious about choosing sustainable textiles, others prioritize labor practices. Here are three sustainable fashion categories:

1. **Rent instead of buying** - You can lease items of clothing, return them when you no longer need them and exchange them for something new.

2. **Resale and consignment** - Clothes can find multiple closets instead of ending up in a landfill. Loads of new people can use them. Thrift stores are an ever-popular place to buy second-hand clothes, and now you can thrift using Wi-Fi on a site called ThredUp. There are more than 35,000 brands to choose from, with up to 90% off. According to the calculations done by ThredUp, if everyone bought one used item instead of a brand new one in a year, 25 billion gallons of water and 449 million pounds of waste would be saved.

3. **Using recycled materials to create something new** - We've all heard that one person's trash is another person's treasure. Garments should ideally be passed down instead of being thrown away. Swap clothes for as long as possible, then use them for quilting projects or as rags. Canyon, an all-terrain sneaker brand, makes shoes entirely from recycled plastic bottles. Every pair uses 3.5 plastic bottles.

Upcycling waste is creative and challenging. Previously upcycling meant turning a pair of old jeans into a skirt, and these days, it's transforming clothes into something edgy, reinvigorating them with new life. The difference between recycling and upcycling is this, recycling is turning an old unused shirt into cleaning rags and upcycling is repurposing them into a one of a kind scarf. People have overflowing closets and they are left with the option of either disposing of or recycling their old clothing. Some people also have an attachment to clothing worn by deceased family members and have a hard time letting go of it. They can redesign and repurpose it to make something new and wear their loved one's clothes.

Another good way to reuse your outfits is to redesign them. Usually, the style of the garment becomes unfashionable, but the fabric does not. Upcycling seems to be a new movement in haute couture and everyone from the rich to young entrepreneurs is getting involved. Upcycling lessens the production of waste which would take thousands of years to break down, it preserves our natural resources and stops pollution, it saves you money by reinventing your old clothes, it preserves your parents' and grandparents' hand-me-downs, and it gives you a customized piece of clothing for yourself. If you keep old clothes long enough, they'll come back as retro fashion.

Fashion trends happen so quickly that there is always unused fabric lying around that can be used in hundreds of ways. Upcycling is a way for textile manufacturers to reuse their waste into something fashionable. It can be turned into paper pulp, rags, or even new garments. While some larger brands have adopted sustainable fashion practices, some have adopted the sustainable concept more as a marketing tool than to actually add value. There is a big difference between using sustainability for marketing and for building a company based on the concept. Contact the store directly if you're not sure whether they are a sustainable business or not. Ask the staff. Cotton and synthetics are harsher on the environment than linen or hemp because the pesticides and insecticides used to grow cotton are dangerous to the environment and to the farmers. Take note of the packaging, an environmentally conscious company will not use bubble wrap or plastic bags. Buy local garments, as they will travel a smaller distance using less energy.

Unfortunately, women between the ages of 25 and 35 reported that they were less concerned with environmental issues than the style and price of their clothes. They also wanted to know where these clothes had come from and who had worn them last. They voiced concerns about hygiene related to upcycled garments as well as the slightly higher price. These are concerns that you will have to contend with if you intend to sell upcycled clothing. Specifically, you will be up against the fast fashion industry.

Twenty items of clothing are manufactured for every person each year. This makes fashion a multi-trillion dollar industry. Fast fashion has fed this industry by making cheap clothes with a very low price tag. The fast fashion ideology shortens fashion cycles and decreases the customers' waiting period. This has increased the number of fashion seasons from 2 major seasons to approximately 100 micro-seasons. Because of this trend, customers are buying around 60% more but keeping the clothes for half the time. This has a tremendous impact on the environment.

Cotton is used 33% more than any other fiber and requires 2,700 liters of water to make a cotton shirt. This is what an average person drinks in 2 ½ years. The clothing industry is projected to skyrocket within the next few years, as an estimated 5.2 billion people enter middle-class lifestyles. While some will adopt new innovative ways that work to be sustainable, many others will be unlikely to change their traditional way of manufacturing. Clothing manufacturers must begin the transformation towards eradicating environmental risks. Companies must first recognize that they are expected to do more than just improve efficiency; they have to manufacture fewer, more durable products.

Selling Your Used Clothing

Are you ready to sell some clothes? How many items of clothing do you have that you are not using anymore? Pants, shoes, belts, and dresses, you probably have plenty of these, and it's time for them to have a brand new home. You can sell your unwanted clothes online if you're willing to put in a bit of work. You can make extra money quickly this way, potentially up to $1,000. Clothes that are fashionable and cute are always in demand, and it's never been easier to sell them. Besides making money, selling your unused clothing can help you organize your life by scaling down and your mornings less stressful, essentially decluttering your life. You can build a sustainable business from selling unwanted or barely used clothes. Here is a list of sites to help you find your fit and that can help you sell your unwanted items of clothing.

1. **ThredUp** - It's so simple, you can order a clean out kit from their site, put all the clothes you want to sell in the bags they supply, and ship it back to them for free. Their second-hand experts will go through what you've sent them. They will take what they want and recycle the rest. It takes a few

weeks before they get back to you with the price, and you can either donate it to a charity or get paid via PayPal. This is an effortless way to sell your clothes without negotiating or taking pictures of your items. ThredUp accepts high-quality women's and children's clothes that are still in good condition.

2. **Poshmark** - This is another easy site to use and is a great place to sell your clothes online. You will need to download the app, take some photos, and then share them. They will take a 20% fee, but for that percentage, you'll get no-hassle shipping. You can sell your clothes quickly, and you can negotiate the price.

3. **eBay** - You can probably sell your clothes on eBay for a lot more money than anywhere else. This site is excellent for rare items and high-end designers. Their fees are also much cheaper than other websites. You have the option to fix the price or auction them off.

4. **Depop** - This app is a bit like eBay and Instagram. It's aimed at teenagers and people in their 20s. Make sure you take great photos and have an excellent description. You can sell anything from

vintage to quirky and unique items. Depop charges 10% on your sales, and they pay you via PayPal.

5. **Facebook Marketplace** - This is another great site for selling used clothing. Use your Facebook account, go to the marketplace icon, list your items, and click on and sell something. You can use this to sell to people in your area. Facebook Marketplace doesn't charge you for your use of their app, so you get to keep all the profits.

6. **Tradesy** - This is perfect if you have more than just clothes to sell. Handbags, accessories, or just about anything will make you some money here. Just make sure that they're all in good condition. They do charge a commission on your sales.

7. **Vinted** - This site is easy to use and is excellent for buyers and sellers. Once you've created an account, you will be able to list all the items you have for free. They have great extra features as well. This is a great way to declutter your closet.

8. **Instagram** - This is perfect for girls who know how social media works, especially those that have a following. You can list your photos for free and you have control over pricing and marketing.

9. **Craigslist** - While this may not be trendy, it is an option. It is reliable and free, so you get to keep all the profits.

10. **Mercari** - This app has been designed to sell anything. It is user friendly and will cost you 10% of your sales.

11. **Rebag** - You can sell your designer handbags on this site. Your handbag must have a brand name on it for it to be considered. Send a photo of your bag, or you can visit them in the store for an assessment. They are quite strict, so check their requirements first. You'll receive a quote if your handbag has been approved.

12. **LePrix** - This is a great site if you have high-end designer items that are in excellent condition. You will be required to go through the authentication process first.

13. **The Real Real** - They work with brands like Prada, Gucci, Louis Vuitton, etc. High-end designer and fashion items. Send your items to them, and they will authenticate, price, and sell your items.

14. **Grailed** - They specialize in men's clothing, which makes it a great place to sell clothes and declutter your closet if you are a man.

15. **VarageSale** - Basically an old fashioned garage sale. You can sell anything and everything here. This app helps you sell in your local area, so there are no shipping fees to worry about. It's easy to use, just post a photo and description of the item and wait for the potential buyer to contact you. VarageSale checks out both buyers and sellers, so it is much safer than Craigslist and it's free.

16. **Material World** - This site works exactly like ThredUp.

You have a list of sites that you can use, but now you need some tips on how to be successful in selling your clothes. Check the clothes in your closet to see what you can sell. Remember, a lot of these sites are quite popular and can become crowded, so you need to stand out from the competition. Here are some easy tips and tricks to get the most out of selling your second-hand clothes.

1. Make sure that the item is worth selling. Take a look at items for sale that are similar to yours to see what people are prepared to pay. Make sure that your price is competitive. You may think that you will get close to what you paid for it, but that's highly unlikely. Before setting a price, take

into consideration the work involved before you list. Don't set your price too low because it may not be worth it.

2. Prepare your clothes by giving them a makeover. Wash and iron them because they've probably been in your closet for a while now.

3. Prepare the stage for sales. People buy with their eyes, so make sure that you use an uncluttered background when you take a photo. Give them an Instagram look by photographing them on a flat surface and always use natural light. Brighten and crop the picture so that it looks exactly like the real item. A wooden hanger will make your clothes look smart.

4. Take photos that will sell your item. Think about what you would look for if you were to buy second-hand clothes online. Take a few photos, at least one front, one back, and a close-up.

5. Add an accurate description and include the brand and the size of the item. Add some personal touches and give your opinion of the item and why you are selling it.

HOME-BASED JOBS & SUSTAINABLE CRAFTS

6. Make sure that you are selling your item when it is trendy and seasonal. No one will buy a swimsuit in the middle of winter.

7. Respond to the customer as soon as possible or straight away if you can. No one likes to wait, and you don't want them to move on to something else.

8. Work your shipping costs into the price. Get estimates for shipping and packaging in advance.

9. Most online apps charge their own fees. Consider this as well, as it will impact your profits.

10. Sell multiple items at once and save yourself some time. Do all steps from 1 - 10 for each item in your batch before uploading your items for sale. You'll sell more items more quickly this way.

With every new season, we're all planning on updating our wardrobes. We are usually running out of closet space and most importantly, money. Many of us suffer from buyer's remorse, so we all probably have clothes that still have the tags on or clothes that we thought were a great buy at the time but turned out to be not so great. You might as well make some money and get rid of some of those unwanted fashion faux pas. Treat yourself and your closet to a fresh new look. You'll be surprised at how many people will pay for the clothes you no longer need.

With the endless online possibilities for selling your clothes, please be aware that there are people out there ready to scam you. Read all the fine print and the site's policies before you commit yourself. If you find that it's just too much work to photograph the clothes before selling them online, then a consignment store is the option for you. Most consignment stores work the same, you take your clothes in, they make you an offer, and you can either accept or decline. A Google search for consignment stores in your area will be a good start. Some popular shops are Clothes Mentor and Plato's Closet. Of course, you can also consider ThredUp, which we mentioned above.

You're probably not going to be getting rich quickly by this method unless you want to dip your hand into the million-dollar second hand and used item businesses. However, try not to give up if your first sales turn out to be difficult. Use this as a learning process and get a system in place. Many people do this, and as long as you don't become discouraged, it can be fun and rewarding.

Chapter 9:
Selling Used Books

Would you like to do your part for sustainable reading and help the environment? Readers know the value of knowledge; we love our books because they allow us to transform ourselves through education. There is something magical about books. We can catch a glimpse into the world around us through our imagination. Our love for books, especially the ones in print form, could be damaging the environment. As responsible citizens, we have to do the right thing.

Over two billion books are printed in the USA each year, and that means about 30 million trees are destroyed. That's enough trees to fill 37,000 football fields, which is equivalent to the size of Washington DC. The manufacturing of paper uses lots of oil and gas; in fact, the world's third-largest user of fossil fuels is the paper industry. Most of the time, books are not read and then passed on to someone else to read and enjoy. Although it would be great if they were, the truth is that over 10 million trees' worth of books ends up destroyed.

When a book is released, thousands of copies are printed at once to bring down the printing cost. In many cases, most of these books are not sold, so they end up being destroyed. They could even be left in a warehouse, never to be used, or remaindered. Remaindered refers to books that have been sold to a discount book store that sells former best-sellers at a discounted price. There are, however, books that made their way to a bookstore but were not sold. Now, bookstores can ask the publisher for a refund, but because of high shipping costs, the bookstore tears off the cover of the book and sends it back alone, leaving the entire book unsellable. These books are pulped, meaning they're recycled into paper. The recycling process isn't very eco-friendly because it takes a lot of electricity and chemicals to break down the paper before it can be used for other products. Each year, 16,000 truckloads of unread books are destroyed. We need to make books more environmentally friendly.

Sustainable Reading

Digital reading is the easiest way to foster sustainable reading and stop the destructive cycle of trees. Even though digital reading devices such as iPads, Kindles, and e-readers do leave a carbon footprint, they have a much lower impact on the environment. We must commit to reduce our carbon footprint and be good stewards of the earth and the environment. These days, you don't even need a Kindle to read on because you can use your phone or laptop. Reading 100 books on your Kindle or phone is far more environmentally friendly than reading those books in print. So as an avid reader, switching to e-books can help the environment.

If you're not a fan of e-books and must have a book to hold and pages to turn, look for sustainable print options. Visit your local library, as this is the most sustainable option. Books that have been lent out over and over again maximize the utility of the resources that go into publishing a book. Build your collection of used books if you don't want to borrow from the library. You can buy used books from online used booksellers or even your local bookstore. Some bookshops offer a buy-back system, which means you will get store credit when you return your used book. You can do your part by donating the books you've read to a charity where they will be reread.

Another sustainable publishing option is print on demand. The POD system prints only the books that have been sold, so a book is printed only when a customer places an order for it. It is then packed and shipped directly to the customer. POD suppliers ensure that they use at least 30% recycled paper when they print their books.

What Types of Books Can You Sell?

If you're looking for a way to make some money on the weekend, then this is for you. Turn your old books into profit. Books have become one of the top-selling online categories, and some publishing companies have even reported higher sales from online sources than from their physical outlets. If you're an entrepreneur who wants to learn how to sell online or someone who has tons of used books that you'd like to rehome, this chapter will guide you into the online book sales business. One of the keys to buying and selling books online is to know how much people are willing to pay for them before you sell them. Just because you can buy a book for $1 does not mean that you should. Only buy a book if you know for sure that you can make some money on it. If you're wondering which books would make you the most money, well, it will depend on what is in demand and how your business is promoted. The four types of books that are usually needed are:

Textbooks - This market is estimated at between $5 billion and $8.5 billion. There is a lot of money that can be made from this. Even though many textbooks are sold on campus, many people still buy and sell them online. If you want to sell your textbooks, that's great, but why not become a "textbook flipper" by buying them and reselling them for a profit? You can start looking at places like garage sales and second-hand stores and ask your family and friends. You might be lucky and find one or two on eBay, Amazon, or even Craigslist. You can sell textbooks almost anywhere, and eBay and Amazon are great online sites that you can list your books on. Other marketplaces are textbook specific. Take a look at the following list: Textbooks.com, BookScouter.com, Chegg.com, CampusBookRentals.com, and AbeBooks.

Modern First Edition Books - These are books that were published in the last 30 or 40 years. They are collectibles for some people, who enjoy these books and authors, and for others, they will pay a higher price for something that may become collectible in the future. Recent first editions are relatively easy to find, as it's the first editions printed many years ago that tend to be rare. The older the first edition is, the higher the profit for you. To determine whether the book is the first edition or not, check for some of these:

1. First Edition or First Published will appear on the copyright page.

2. A number line is present, 987654321, if a 1 is present, this will be the first edition. For the second printing, the 1 will be removed, and the lowest number will be 2.

3. The date appears on both the title page and the copyright page.

eBay is a great place to sell your modern first edition books.

Out of Print Used Books - These are your regular run of the mill books. There's not too much money in them. You will be able to find them in any bookshop or thrift store.

Collectible and Antique Books - You can use a book scanner app, which will give you the potential profit margin for a book, especially if you're selling on a marketplace.

How to Promote and Sell Your Books

In order for you to sell books online, you need to set up an independent bookstore. This way, you will maximize profits without having to pay out commission on your sales. Shopify is ideal, and it supports a wide range of templates. Shopify works great on mobile devices, giving you the opportunity to sell to mobile shoppers. Some legalities must be taken care of when starting an online business. You must register your business's name and get a tax number, as you don't want complications later on. You can be fined for running a business without registration. You will also need to register a domain name for your bookstore.

Once you've done all that, the next step is to promote your bookstore and expose your brand. A marketing strategy is beneficial to any entrepreneur, as you can send potential customers a newsletter and links to your products. Upload good quality images of your products, run competitions, and share discount coupons. Connections with social media influencers will give you an added advantage, as you can get them to review a book or share your store link on their platforms. Social media influencers can be found on Facebook, Instagram and YouTube. Keep up your momentum when you're promoting your bookstore. After Google, YouTube is the second biggest search engine in the world. So posting a detailed video about your bookstore on YouTube is a great way to generate interest. The next step would be to find a wholesale book supplier. Buying stock at a wholesale price will give you a good margin, and you will be able to get discounts from them after a while. You can get all genres of books from these suppliers:

1. **Used Wholesale Books** - They have about 7 million books for sale at any time. They also have a wide variety of wholesale, fiction and kids books, which are in excellent condition to buy.

2. **Bulk Bookstore** - They offer up to 55% discounts with free shipping. Use their

online catalog to check the availability of books or you can send them your list to get a quote. You can get anything from first edition books to textbooks from Bulk Bookstore.

3. **Book Depot** - They offer books for 75% - 90% off the list price. Their books are genuine and in excellent condition. The book categories range from philosophy to antiques, from games to medical. Blow out books are sold at a fraction of the cost, and if you don't mind dusting, it can help you save even more money.

4. **Better World Books** - They offer media stock and bulk books ranging from religious texts to best sellers. They have a large variety of leather-bound and vintage books. Books are sold by a box, a pallet, or a container so the price will depend on what you're buying.

You can find amazing books at yard sales and offline distributors as well. You could buy stock for 10¢ a book this way. Craigslist and eBay have first edition books as well as textbooks for sale. All of these options will allow you to get books that you can resell on another marketplace for a profit.

Of course, you can resell your books on Amazon, eBay, or Craigslist, which we have discussed in previous chapters. However, there are many other websites and brick and mortar stores that you can use to sell your books. Here are the 5 best places to sell hardcovers, paperbacks, and textbooks:

1. **Half Price Books** - This is the USA's biggest family-owned bookstore, with over 120 stores. Take your books to one of their outlets to get an appraisal, and Half Priced Books will make you an offer.

2. **Book Scouter.com** - You will be able to get a good idea as to what different companies are willing to pay for your books. Prices always change, so don't wait too long to make the sale.

3. **AbeBooks Buyback** - Consider using this service to sell your textbooks. They will beat the price of the local college bookstore. Don't send them damaged books because they will be recycled and you won't get anything out of it.

4. **Powell's Books** - You can take your books to one of their stores or use their website, get an appraisal, and sell your books. They work similarly to Half Price Books. The books must be in pristine condition before they take them. Check their website to learn what issues would make them reject a book.

However, Powell's will give you a store credit if they take your books.

5. **Textbooks.com** - This company not only buys used textbooks, but they also sell them to students and guarantee them cashback on certain books. You can sell all your college textbooks on this site.

You will need a solid knowledge of self-publishing if you've written a few books and would like to sell them online. Some platforms can help you with this, one such example is:

Blurb - Writers learn how to sell their books in various formats online. You can create, promote, and publish your book. You will also be able to change your book into a photo book, trade book, magazine, e-books, etc. Blurb will handle shipping for you. Pick a template and upload your book, it's that easy. Blurb's Adobe InDesign allows you to build your own template, but there are loads of templates to complement any industry. Now that your book is ready, go to "Sell and Distribute" and set the price. Get the word out about your book, market and promote it on all social media platforms. Hand out free copies and ask for reviews. Blurb will send you a payment on any sales at the end of the month.

Amazon - You can design your books using a third-party website and sell your books here on

Amazon. Give Amazon your ISBN and your book will be ready for self-publishing. After you've set up your author profile, you can set the price of the book. Amazon does charge a fee to prepare the book, so add this to your price. If you're selling third party books, this is relatively easy to do, send the stock to Amazon and they will take care of the shipping and handling for you.

Tips for First-Timers

Here are some tips if you're selling books for the first time. List your books properly and be transparent about the condition of the books. Mention whether there are missing pages, highlighted passages, or any writing in the books. If you're not upfront about the condition of the book, the buyer may reject your book altogether. But if you are honest, they know what to expect and will probably just decrease their offer or only make an offer if they don't mind the condition. You'll get positive feedback and make loads of money.

If your books are in great condition, make sure that you package them carefully before shipping them off. It is your responsibility to make sure that the books arrive in one piece and without damage, otherwise you are likely to end up with negative reviews and refund requests. You can save yourself some cash by getting the buyer to pay for shipping.

If you're considering selling old or used magazines, this is a tricky one, as you may not make any money for the effort you'll put in. You're actually better off just donating them to a retirement home or recycling them.

Another useful tip is to download the bookscouter.com app. If you have books to sell and you're not sure what the going rate is for them, this will be your saving grace. Just enter the ISBN into the app, and it will show what people are willing to pay for the book. Download the free mobile app, which will be quite handy when you're browsing through thrift stores or yard and estate sales. You will be able to enter the ISBN to see the current selling price, so you don't miss an opportunity to make a good profit.

The end... almost!

Reviews are not easy to come by.

As an independent author with a tiny marketing budget, I rely on readers, like you, to leave a short review on Amazon.

Even if it's just a sentence or two!

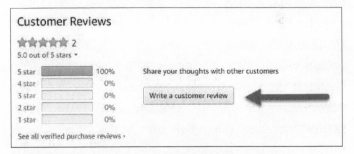

So if you enjoyed the book, please...

Leave a brief review on Amazon.

I am very appreciative for your review as it truly makes a difference.

Thank you from the bottom of my heart for purchasing this bookand reading it to the end.

Chapter 10:
Candle Making

Candle making is a wonderful world of beauty and color. One where you make money and have some fun while doing it. In medieval times, chandlery, or candle making, was actually a rather masculine skill. Everyone relied on candles then, from businesses to homes and churches. Candles were made from wax or tallow, which is the fat from cows and sheep. It was a rather lucrative profession then as light was a necessity to all kingdoms and villages. Candles may be simple, but they are hugely significant. They were a luxury item given as gifts during festivals. Candles were also used in spiritual worship, with many different cultures using their own methods and products. The Qin dynasty used beeswax and whale fat for their candles. Candles in India were made with cinnamon and yak butter, which were the world's first scented candles. The indigenous people of North America used candlefish or smelt fish as a source of lighting. This was great for sustained light but had a very unpleasant odor. The first commercial candle makers were born after the fall of the Roman Empire when there was a shortage of oil for oil lamps. Once the lightbulb was invented, the need for candles dwindled.

However, the popularity of candles has grown in recent years. Although candles aren't a necessity, they do add a romantic ambiance to any room. Depending on what you're going for, candles have lovely scents like sandalwood and bourbon. Homemade candles cost a fraction of a store-bought one, and they burn and smell just as good as the expensive kind. This natural process won't take you more than a few hours and will make great gifts for friends and family. There are loads of different types of candles out there, but the easiest one for a beginner is a container candle. These are candles that come in mason jars or containers, and the best part is you don't need specialized tools or equipment to make them. In this chapter, you will find not only inspiration but also actionable steps to embark on your very own candle making journey. This chapter covers everything you need to know, from the tools that you need to add your own personal touches to the candles.

You can start your very own candle making business with just a few easy steps. You will need to decide what type of candle you would like to make and what recipe will work best. There is a difference between making and creating, and the goal is to create natural and organic candles. For you to create, you must understand how each ingredient reacts to each other and how they interact. To make your business successful, your product must stand out; it must be unique. Lots of local stores sell candles, so you won't have a business if you're making carbon copies.

However, you can look at the candle industry for inspiration. Look at what types of candles are being produced already. Candlemakers and perfumers have joined forces to give us luxury fragrant candles. Other companies are embedding small prizes in their candles, with a small chance to win something valuable. These candles can cost you anything from $50 or more. You may be interested in making something like this, or you may identify a missing niche in the market. Maybe there is a smell combination you would like that isn't readily available, or perhaps you have a particular candle aesthetic in mind.

Many people love the effect of the warm glow that the candles give off, making their homes cozy and comfortable. Soy candle making is another inexpensive method that leaves ample room for your creativity to run free. You can buy supplies for a dozen homemade candles for the cost of a few store-bought ones. It's so easy once you get started. However, it can get complicated at the same time. You can make a few candles within an hour with a few supplies, but getting the perfect result can be a bit tricky. We will go over a summary of the candle-making process and give more detailed options and recipes. Over time you will be able to tweak and adjust the recipe to suit your needs and even come up with your very own unique blends of fragrances.

When making your candles, be creative in choosing a candle container, use mason jars, drinking glasses, mugs, tins, ceramic flower pots, teacups, or even small bowls. Just make sure that they are heat safe. To determine how much wax you will need for your chosen container, fill it with water, then pour it into a measuring cup. This way, you won't waste any wax. Next, choose the wick size. Then weigh in the correct amount of wax on the scale. For every 1 ounce of fluid, you will need 1 ounce in weight of wax. Weighing out the fragrances can be tricky because the properties vary one from the other. Basically, you will need 1 ounce of fragrance per 1 pound wax. You can adjust this as you go if you're not satisfied with the scent.

Getting Started

Let's talk about the supplies and tools you will need to get started and then go over the steps in more detail. Because the startup cost for candle making is quite low, you will be creating several candles with only a few supplies and tools.

You will need the following supplies:

- Heat-proof jars and other candle containers
- Pre-waxed and pre-tabbed wicks
- Soy wax flakes or any other wax of your choice
- Superglue
- A double boiler or a large pot to use as a double boiler
- Melting pot, large glass, heat-proof pitcher, or bowl
- Wooden mixing spoon or spatula
- Scale
- Thermometer
- Masking tape or old pens
- Fragrant essential oils
- Paper towels

Wax: This the primary ingredient of any candle. There are three types of candle making wax for you to choose from:

- **Paraffin:** This has been used for hundreds of years; it's cheap and can be easily colored and scented. This traditional wax is petroleum-based and toxic, so you should get an all-natural alternative product.

- **Soy:** This is new on the market and is quickly becoming popular. It is made with soybean oil but is sometimes blended with paraffin, palm wax, or beeswax. You can also add color and scent to soy wax.

- **Beeswax:** Bees produce this as a byproduct of honey making. This is entirely natural and gold in color, with a slight sweet scent to it. Beeswax is considered the oldest ingredient in candle making; some of these candles were found in the pyramids. However, you won't be able to add to its scent and it is quite expensive.

Waxes for candle making usually come in small pellet forms, which makes it easier to melt. If the wax does come in large blocks, cut it into small manageable pieces. A must for candle making is a double boiler or large pot in which you can melt your wax. There are hundreds of fragrant oils to choose from and use. You can choose from essential oils or fragrances specially formulated for use in candle making. Candlescience.com has scents such as Fireside, Buttered Rum, Whiskey and Apples, and Maple Bourbon. The wicks are also an important part of the candle. Wicks are sized, small, medium, and large. The length does not matter as you can trim it to your desired length.

Get some containers: mugs, mason jars, shot glasses, or anything else that can be used to house a candle. Just make sure they can withstand the heat of a lighted candle. Another tool you should have is a thermometer because fragrances are added when the wax reaches a specific temperature. You will also need a spatula or spoon to stir the wax. The process for all wax types is roughly the same. Now we can move on to the really exciting part of making our very own candle in a container. Remember, safety first! You will be working with very hot wax.

Step 1. Prepare the work area.

Be prepared for the wax to get on everything, and you will probably only find out where once it's dry. Use old newspapers or paper towels to cover the work area. It's a quick process once you get started, so have everything you need close at hand.

Step 2. Melt the wax.

Melt the wax in a double boiler. It usually takes about 10 - 15 minutes to melt. Use the spatula to stir or break up the bigger chunks. The ideal temperature can vary by wax type and ranges from 120 to 180 degrees Fahrenheit. It is best to check the information for the specific wax you purchase.

Step 3: Adhere the wick to the container.

Some wicks come with a built-in sticker that you can use to stick to the bottom of your container. However, most don't, so you can use superglue or the old candle makers trick of dipping the metal tab into the liquid wax and quickly sticking it into the center of the container. The wax will harden after a few minutes, and the wick will be stuck to the bottom.

Step 4: Add fragrant oils.

Once the wax has melted until liquid, add your preferred scent to the double boiler. The temperature can also vary by wax type for this step. In the case of soy wax, add fragrance at 175 to 185 degrees Fahrenheit. Stir to distribute the fragrance. Different types of wax require different amounts of fragrance, so take note of the instructions that come with the wax.

Step 5: Pour into the container.

When the scented wax has cooled to about 130 - 140 degrees Fahrenheit, pour it into your preferred container. Lightly hold on to the wick so that it doesn't move. Leave a little wax in the double boiler for later.

Step 6. Secure the wick.

The wick may move around in the wax and could harden off-center. To ensure that this does not happen use some old pens and secure the wick between them on top of the container. Once the wick is secure, you can remove the pens. If the wick is off-center, it won't burn properly.

Step 7. Cool and top off.

Once the wax cools and settles, you may find that a sinkhole has formed in the middle. Reheat the leftover wax and fill in the hole. Add enough just to fill in the depression and for a smooth finish. Too much wax may cause another sinkhole to form.

Step 9. Trim the wick.

Trim the wick to about a ¼ of an inch. If the wick is too long, it will burn too hot and too big.

Step 10. Clean up.

The easiest way to clean up any wax that has spilled is to wipe it up while it's still in liquid form. If it does harden, you can easily scrape the wax off the surface of your tools, countertops, etc. You can then wash normally.

Things to remember:

Allow the candles to cool for at least 24 hours before lighting them. Ensure that the surface that the candle is on is stable. Keep the candles away from children and pets. Never leave a burning candle near anything combustible or unattended. It may take some time to get the desired scent or for it to be perfectly smooth. Take heart that with every batch of candles you make, you're one step closer to perfection.

How to Start Selling Your Homemade Candles Online

Homemade candles are in much higher demand than mass-produced ones. They're easy to sell and cheaper to make. What better reasons could there be for you to sell them online and from home? Selling candles online will be your entry into the world of e-commerce and running a successful online business from home. You can build a strong marketing strategy with some interesting facts about the candle industry.

Also, consider the reasons people would purchase a candle when designing your business. People usually buy candles as home decor elements, to reduce stress, and for aromatherapy. They use candles to make their homes cozy and comfortable, usually placing them in bedrooms and living rooms, sometimes even in their bathrooms. The fragrance and how the candles look influences customers' purchasing decisions. Candles make great gifts for birthdays, housewarmings, and thank you gifts. Men and women both appreciate candles as gifts, making candles quite a popular item.

With that in mind, you want to ensure that there is a market for what you're selling. Do market research to determine which of the below candle components you can use and categories you can target to maximize your sales.

Scented or Aromatherapy Candles - These are used to bring a fragrant smell to their homes. They are bought for special occasions. There is a wide variety of scents that you can use:

- Vanilla and nutmeg
- Mandarine
- Sandalwood
- Tobacco
- Lavender
- Peach

The list goes on and on. Aromatherapy candles have hints of essential oil that help soothe the mind and the body. You can buy all you need from Amazon or from your local supply store.

Coloring - Each coloring has its pros and cons, and there are many types that you can add to your candles. Listed here a few choices as well as how well they work:

a) Color Blocks - These provide the richest color and are by far the cheapest option to color your candles. Even though they are very cost-effective, it is difficult to get the precise color you want every single time. Try using color blocks for dark-colored candles only.

b) Liquid Dyes - These are absolutely perfect for achieving the shade of color you are looking for. However, all liquid dyes have a hint of a chemical smell.

c) Color Chips - These are slightly overpriced and you may have a problem with achieving the color you're looking for. Give it a go and see if you like it.

d) Crayons - If you're making a few candles to try out the process, these can be a good option. They are, however, not something you should consider if you're making high-quality candles.

Candle Additives - Additives are used to enhance the quality of a candle. Many candle makers use this method, and although this is not recommended, you once again should decide whether this is a good option for you. Here is a list of additives:

a) Vybar - This is used to enhance the scent of the candle. It produces a marbled look on the top and gives the entire candle an opaque look. It will help you create a really nice looking candle.

b) UV Light Protectors - First off, these are expensive. UV light protectors ensure that the candle's natural color is maintained because otherwise, the color will fade if left for too long in the sun. This will be an excellent investment if you're planning on selling them wholesale.

c) Petrolatum - Add some of this to your wax if the wax you're using does not hold to the sides of your containers. Petrolatum will absorb more fragrance but will not burn cleanly. It should be noted that this is a petroleum byproduct and may not be desirable for eco-friendly candles.

d) Crisco Shortening - Believe it or not, Crisco shortening is great for a quality candle. It has several benefits, as it decreases wet spots and helps absorb the scent. However, some believe that the fumes from burning Crisco can be toxic, so it is up to you whether you would like to use it.

Selling Decorative Candles - When making decorative candles, how the candles look is most important. People buy these to decorate their rooms. They come in so many different shapes and colors. Search online to get an idea of what is in demand and for inspiration.

Soy and Vegan Candles - These are made from soybean extract and are in very high demand. They burn longer and cleanly. Soy candles sell for a higher price so you can give this one a go.

There are lots of other types of candles that you can make and sell. While you explore the opportunities to sell candles, always check whether they are in demand before you commit. You need something unique that will intrigue the online shoppers. Before you can start making candles, you must think about how you're going to sell them. You can sell your candles on popular marketplaces such as eBay, Amazon, or Etsy, but if you are serious about this, why not start your own online store? Alternatively, you can work on your website while selling on these marketplaces. It is important to establish your online presence and stand out if you want to do better than your competitors within the first year of your business. The process is straightforward, whether you want to make a bit of extra income or if you want a successful online business. However, getting your product noticed is the hard part.

Making candles and starting a website is pretty easy; the tricky part is marketing. So, what are the best marketing strategies to sell candles online?

Whichever platform you plan on using to sell your candles online, you must first let your customers know about them. You can run a Facebook ad or make an Instagram account. This is the easiest and cheapest way to get your product noticed. These platforms have a massive audience for you to tap into. You don't have to wait until you have a finished product, start now. Add videos that show your progress and start a blog. This will generate interest in your business even before it gets off the ground. Include links to your products to increase traffic and most importantly, sales.

Candle making can be very profitable if you can make a great candle. Always continue to better your craft even if you start making money immediately. Have an effective distribution system, and try to get your candles into local stores as well. The demand for candles is steadily increasing, and that presents a wonderful opportunity for you to generate interest and demand for your product. Remember, any business can be a good business. The amount of sales you make is totally up to you.

Starting a candle making business is a perfect example of how you can turn your hobby into a moneymaker either full-time or part-time. One of the hottest topics around the world these days is "Going Green." "Green" is associated with products and or services that are effective in promoting environmental protection. The candle market is full of renewable raw materials. Many people are choosing green candles that use beeswax or soy wax, and both are eco-friendly. Glass candle containers are also considered green, as they can be recycled and reused. Your marketing strategy could look like this, the wax is a natural product, and the glassware is 100% recycled glass. This will appeal to everyone who is environmentally conscious. The wick is also a natural product, and it's 100% cotton. This type of marketing opens the doors to a rapidly growing segment of customers, and it helps out the planet!

Conclusion

I hope that you gained a better understanding of how our economy works as you've journeyed through this book. What is necessary to be successful and to have fulfillment? Many topics have been covered in this book, from economics to entrepreneurship. The many fundamental economic concepts we've explained hopefully no longer seem mysterious and will guide your decisions as you form your own business.

I do hope that this book has been an eye-opener in terms of how everyday economics works. It's hard to get people excited about economics and to get them to think about how economics can be applied in everyday life. Economics puts a theory behind our daily actions. Economics, in a nutshell, is how we, as consumers use the limited amount of resources we have available to maximize our satisfaction by buying the products we will find most useful. It deals with the consumption of these products, as well as how the products are priced. You now understand why price is important and how it can be used strategically.

There are also many subheadings and different categories that fall under the economics title. You can see how human behavior influences people's purchasing decisions and how entrepreneurs can use this information to inform their marketing decisions. It can make you think about why you pay what you do for your groceries, perhaps even understanding the part we all play in the price structures. We, the consumers, define economics, and we can use this in our business strategies to bring us favorable results. The psychology behind the pricing system and human behavior is something astounding. The aim of explaining this is so that you can go into your dream venture armed with a wealth of knowledge and insights that very few entrepreneurs have. An entrepreneur has rarely been formally educated in economic matters. They are creative and full of boundless energy ready to take on the world, the business world that is, without giving any thought to the inner workings of the economy.

The business world has been turned on its head during the last few years. Almost everyone from the layman to the world's richest man is constantly reminded that we are responsible for destroying our planet. We have to act and act fast if we want to preserve and restore our beautiful planet. Entrepreneurs again are at the forefront, with their new ways of thinking and their positive business principles, which make the rest of the business world sit up and take notice. They are pushing boundaries, yet remaining true to ethical and sustainable methods. Entrepreneurship is slowly shifting the business landscape. With new technologies released almost daily and with customers looking for niche markets, it can be challenging to keep up. New businesses must embrace the change and keep up to date with what is unique in the industry. Have an edge against your competitors and keep your business moving successfully forward.

The internet is a great place to start generating an additional or alternate income. Digital entrepreneurship is one way of starting your own business with a small amount of funds. Even though digital entrepreneurship requires quite a bit of time and effort in the beginning, the rewards make it worthwhile once it gains momentum. Hopefully, you will use the tips and advice given throughout this book to implement successful marketing strategies and avoid common mistakes. You will be able to make wiser decisions in your own company. There are hundreds and thousands of dollars to be made through genuine money-making opportunities. With hard work and through developing yourself, you will turn whatever you call a hobby into something extremely lucrative. Be eco-friendly and fashion-forward. Remember that repetition is no longer a sin, and you don't need to buy new clothes.

Wasting should never be an option for anyone and any business. The business of selling used books online will work well for those who have a love for the written word, for those who love old and antique books, and for those who love going to estate and yard sales. You can turn that small business idea of yours into a sustainable source of additional income.

I sincerely hope that you have found inspiration in this book to become part of the change that the world needs. There is no better time than the present to change the world. To know that you can have a positive impact on our planet and to create an income stream is literally a dream come true for many. With many inspiring examples of successful people who have tried what you're about to try and have become successful, use these examples and the tried and tested strategies to create great sustainable products. Connect and network with like-minded business associates and potential customers and become part of this amazing movement.

Starting your own business is not as easy as it seems. However, the benefits far outweigh the effort and hard work it takes to launch your business. Remember that what you're building will give you a source of pride and achievement. You will learn new and exciting skills, be independent, and follow your passion. You will be able to create more jobs and make lots of money.

Do what you love. Be patient, and don't give up even if the first results are discouraging. Learn how to make money and how to save money. Support the planet and your community. Live a healthy life and live the life you've always dreamed of.

References

1.1 What Is Economics, and Why Is It Important? – Principles of Economics. (2015). Opentextbc.Ca. https://opentextbc.ca/principlesofeconomics/chapter/1-1-what-is-economics-and-why-is-it-important/

1.2 Microeconomics and Macroeconomics – Principles of Economics. (2019). Opentextbc.Ca. https://opentextbc.ca/principlesofeconomics/chapter/1-2-microeconomics-and-macroeconomics/

5.3 Elasticity and Pricing – Principles of Economics. (2011). Opentextbc.Ca. https://opentextbc.ca/principlesofeconomics/chapter/5-3-elasticity-and-pricing/

6 Essential Behavioral Economics Principles for Business | Brandtrust. (2018, April 18). Brandtrust. http://brandtrust.com/behavioral-economics/

A beginners' guide to aquaponics. (2018, May 11). Thefishsite.Com. https://thefishsite.com/articles/a-beginners-guide-to-aquaponics

A Complete Guide to Aquaponic Gardening. (2018). Green and Vibrant. https://www.greenandvibrant.com/aquaponic-gardening

Abadie, M.-J. (2020). The Everything Candlemaking Book: Create Homemade Candles in Housewarming Colors, Interesting Shapes, and Appealing Scents (Everything®) - Kindle edition by Abadie, Marie-Jeanne. Crafts, Hobbies & Home Kindle eBooks @ Amazon.com. Amazon.Com.

https://www.amazon.com/Everything-Candlemaking-Book-House-Warming-Interesting-ebook/dp/B005I5EL2A/ref=sr_1_5?crid=2IPL57477M FTZ&dchild=1&keywords=candle+making&qid=15884 87798&s=digital-text&sprefix=candle%2Cdigital-text%2C239&sr=1-5

Amadeo, K. (2020, February 15). Where's the Best Standard of Living? Depends Who You Ask. The Balance. https://www.thebalance.com/standard-of-living-3305758

Art. (2019a, May 14). How To Make Your Own Candles at Home | The Art of Manliness. The Art of Manliness. https://www.artofmanliness.com/articles/diy-chandlery-how-to-make-your-own-candles/

Balram, S. (2018, June 9). Reject, revamp, repeat! Why fashion upcycling is now an A-list pursuit. The Economic Times. https://economictimes.indiatimes.com/magazines/pan ache/why-fashion-upcycling-is-now-an-a-list-pursuit/articleshow/64523807.cms?from=mdr

Basic Economic Lessons that Growth Entrepreneurs Should Heed. (2011, August 20). Edward Lowe Foundation. https://edwardlowe.org/basic-economic-lessons-that-growth-entrepreneurs-should-heed-2/

Baumann, K. (2011, October 18). What's the importance of price elasticity of demand to the government? | eNotes. ENotes. https://www.enotes.com/homework-help/whats-importance-price-elasticity-demand-285809

Bensonhoff, K. (2019, August 13). The Online Future of Entrepreneurship: A New Age. Business 2 Community. https://www.business2community.com/startups/the-online-future-of-entrepreneurship-a-new-age-02239805

Biddle, D. (1993, November). Recycling for Profit: The New Green Business Frontier. Harvard Business Review. https://hbr.org/1993/11/recycling-for-profit-the-new-green-business-frontier

Bratskeir, K. (2019, September 12). Your complete guide to sustainable fashion—the movement disrupting the industry. Ideas. https://www.wework.com/ideas/worklife/your-complete-guide-to-sustainable-fashion-the-movement-disrupting-the-industry

Brooke, N. (2020). Aquaponics for Beginners: How to Build your own Aquaponic Garden that will Grow Organic Vegetables - Kindle edition by Brooke, Nick. Crafts, Hobbies & Home Kindle eBooks @ Amazon.com. Amazon.Com. https://www.amazon.com/Aquaponics-Beginners-Aquaponic-Organic-Vegetables-ebook/dp/B07KXG7BQ6/ref=sr_1_8?dchild=1&keywords=sustainable+money+making&qid=1588427109&s=digital-text&sr=1-8

Burnett, G. (2018, March 1). Upcycling - An Absolute Beginner's Guide. Georgina Burnett. https://www.georginaburnett.com/upcycling-beginners-guide/

Chladek, N. (2019, November 6). The Importance of Business Sustainability Strategies | HBS Online. Business Insights - Blog. https://online.hbs.edu/blog/post/business-sustainability-strategies

Davis, R. (2020, January 19). Aquaponics System Design, Aquaponics DIY. Grow Food Guide.

https://growfoodguide.com/aquaponics/what-is-the-best-aquaponics-system-design/

Dillehay, J. (2020). Start a Creative Recycling Side Hustle: 101 Ideas for Making Money from Sustainable Crafts Consumers Crave - Kindle edition by Dillehay, James. Arts & Photography Kindle eBooks @ Amazon.com. Amazon.Com. https://www.amazon.com/Start-Creative-Recycling-Side-Hustle-ebook/dp/B084DCPWKW/ref=sr_1_2?dchild=1&keywords=sustainable+money+making&qid=1588427109&s=digital-text&sr=1-2

Drew, D., & Yehounme, G. (2017). The Apparel Industry's Environmental Impact in 6 Graphics | World Resources Institute. Wri.Org. https://www.wri.org/blog/2017/07/apparel-industrys-environmental-impact-6-graphics

Firms in competitive markets - Baripedia. (n.d.). Baripedia.Org. Retrieved May 23, 2020, from https://baripedia.org/wiki/Firms_in_competitive_markets

Green Candlemaking: Environmentally Friendly Options | Candlewic. (n.d.). Www.Candlewic.Com. Retrieved May 23, 2020, from https://www.candlewic.com/education/shopping-help/green-candle-making/green-candlemaking-environmentally-friendly-options/page.aspx?id=1727

Hall, M. (2019). What Is Purchasing Power Parity—PPP? Investopedia. https://www.investopedia.com/updates/purchasing-power-parity-ppp/

Hatchett, F. (2019, October 12). How to Sell Books Online and 5 Places to Sell Them! Ecom Elites | Best Shopify &

Drop Shipping Training Course!
https://ecomelites.com/how-to-sell-books-online/

How profitable is a candle-making business? - Quora.
(n.d.). Www.Quora.Com. Retrieved May 23, 2020,
from https://www.quora.com/How-profitable-is-a-
candle-making-business

How to Sell Candles from Home - Online Business Startup
Guide. (2019, October 17). EcommerceBuff.
https://ecommercebuff.com/how-to-sell-candles-
from-home/

Instructables. (2012, January 24). Small DIY Aquaponics
System. Instructables; Instructables.
https://www.instructables.com/id/Small-DIY-
Aquaponics-System/

Investopedia. (n.d.). The Top 6 Benefits Of Starting A
Home-Based Business. Forbes. Retrieved May 23,
2020, from
https://www.forbes.com/sites/investopedia/2011/06/
27/the-top-6-benefits-of-starting-a-home-based-
business/#10bddbdf7c72

Kahneman Daniel (2011) *Thinking, Fast and Slow*. New
York: Farrar, Straus and Giroux.

Kamleitner, B., Thürridl, C., & Martin, B. A. S. (2019). A
Cinderella Story: How Past Identity Salience Boosts
Demand for Repurposed Products. Journal of
Marketing, 83(6), 002224291987215.
https://doi.org/10.1177/0022242919872156

Kenton, W. (2019). Behavioral Economics. Investopedia.
https://www.investopedia.com/terms/b/behavioraleco
nomics.asp

Kirzner, I. M. (n.d.). Market Theory and the Price System. Https://Www.Mises.at/Static/Literatur/Buch/Kirzner-Market-Theory-and-the-Price-System.Pdf

Koch, R. (2018, March 16). The Chicago School of Behavioral Psychology. https://www.thechicagoschool.edu/insight/business/everyday-examples-of-behavioral-economics/

Kramer, L. (2019). How Does the Law of Supply and Demand Affect Prices? Investopedia. https://www.investopedia.com/ask/answers/033115/how-does-law-supply-and-demand-affect-prices.asp

Legi, C. (2019, July 1). How To Create Sustainable Fashion From Recycled Clothing. Www.Forbes.Com. https://www.digitalistmag.com/improving-lives/2019/07/01/how-to-create-sustainable-fashion-from-recycled-clothing-06199289

Loannou, L., & Serafeim, G. (2019, February 11). Yes, Sustainability Can Be a Strategy. Harvard Business Review. https://hbr.org/2019/02/yes-sustainability-can-be-a-strategy

Max. (2019b, July 8). 15 DIY Aquaponic Plans You Can Actually Build. Green and Vibrant. https://www.greenandvibrant.com/aquaponic-plans

Meyers, G. J. (2014, April). Designing and Selling Recycled Fashion: Acceptance of Upcycled Secondhand Clothes by Female Consumers, Age 25 to 65. *North Dakota State University*. Https://Library.Ndsu.Edu/Ir/Bitstream/Handle/10365/23189/Meyers_Designing%20and%20Selling%20Recycled%20Fashion.Pdf?Sequence=1.

Per Bylund. (2015, December 21). Theory to Practice: 5 Ways Economic Theory Directly Affects a Small

Business. Business.Com; business.com.
https://www.business.com/articles/theory-to-practice-
5-ways-economic-theory-directly-affects-your-small-
business/

Petro, G. (2019, February 8). Upcycling Your Way To
Sustainability. Forbes.
https://www.forbes.com/sites/gregpetro/2019/02/08/
upcycling-your-way-to-sustainability/

Posner, M. H. (2014, September 5). What Is Business
Sustainability And Why Is It Important? - GE. GE
Reports.
https://www.ge.com/reports/post/96692402429/why-
it-pays-for-businesses-to-boost-sustainability/

Radcliffe, B. (2019). A Practical Look At Microeconomics.
Investopedia.
https://www.investopedia.com/articles/economics/08
/understanding-microeconomics.asp

Sullivan, K. (2018, February 13). Sustainable Reading and
Publishing: How You Can Do Your Part to Help the
Environment. TCK Publishing.
https://www.tckpublishing.com/sustainable-reading-
and-publishing/

Thangavelu, P. (2020, April 2). How Microeconomics
Affects Everyday Life. Investopedia.
https://www.investopedia.com/articles/personal-
finance/032615/how-microeconomics-affects-
everyday-life.asp

Tarasin, I. (2019, March 29). A beginner's guide to
upcycling | Lifestyle. Www.Lifestyle.Com.Au.
https://www.lifestyle.com.au/diy/a-beginners-guide-
to-upcycling.aspx

The Editors of Encyclopedia Britannica. (2013). Distribution of wealth and income | economics. In Encyclopædia Britannica. https://www.britannica.com/topic/distribution-of-wealth-and-income

To, C. (2009, June 16). 10 Principles of Economics. Wikiversity.Org; Wikimedia Foundation, Inc. https://en.wikiversity.org/wiki/10_Principles_of_Economics

Ultimate Aquaponics Beginner's Guide. (2019, October 29). Go Green Aquaponics. https://gogreenaquaponics.com/blogs/news/ultimate-aquaponics-beginners-guide

Upcycled Clothing: No longer on the fringes of fashion, but now fashion forward -. (2016, April 7). Mannequin Madness Blog. https://blog.mannequinmadness.com/2016/04/upcycled-clothing-no-longer-on-the-fringes-of-fashion-but-now-fashion-forward/

Vukovic, D. (2018, January 17). Complete Guide to Aquaponic Gardening. Primal Survivor. https://www.primalsurvivor.net/aquaponic-gardening/

Wikipedia Contributors. (2019a, January 14). Perfect competition. Wikipedia; Wikimedia Foundation. https://en.wikipedia.org/wiki/Perfect_competition

Wikipedia Contributors. (2019b, February 15). Sustainable business. Wikipedia; Wikimedia Foundation. https://en.wikipedia.org/wiki/Sustainable_business

Wikipedia Contributors. (2019c, February 28). Supply and demand. Wikipedia; Wikimedia Foundation. https://en.wikipedia.org/wiki/Supply_and_demand

Wikipedia Contributors. (2019d, March 7). Microeconomics. Wikipedia; Wikimedia Foundation. https://en.wikipedia.org/wiki/Microeconomics

Wikipedia Contributors. (2019e, March 23). Behavioral economics. Wikipedia; Wikimedia Foundation. https://en.wikipedia.org/wiki/Behavioral_economics

Wikipedia Contributors. (2019f, May 1). Purchasing power parity. Wikipedia; Wikimedia Foundation. https://en.wikipedia.org/wiki/Purchasing_power_pari ty

Wikipedia Contributors. (2019g, October 10). Information asymmetry. Wikipedia; Wikimedia Foundation. https://en.wikipedia.org/wiki/Information_asymmetr y

Wolla, S. A. (2017). Why Are Some Countries Rich and Others Poor? | St. Louis Fed. Stlouisfed.Org. https://doi.org/https://files.stlouisfed.org/research/p ublications/page1-econ/2017/09/01/why-are-some-countries-rich-and-others-poor_SE.pdf

Discover the ESSENTIAL CONCEPTS OF ECONOMICS that everyone needs to know within 7-minutes

This 7-minute video will give you a powerful edge over everyone else by:

- Discovering how to <u>leverage economic tools</u>

- Making you <u>understand our spending habits</u>

- <u>Predicting</u> economic <u>human behavior</u>

- <u>Understanding the markets</u> and the macro economy

Made in the USA
Middletown, DE
04 January 2021